Fiddler along the Cabot Trail, Cape Breton Island, Nova Scotia

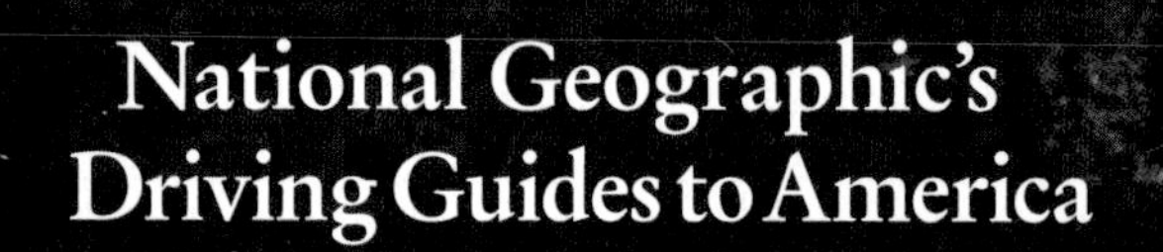

National Geographic's Driving Guides to America

Canada

Prepared by
The Book Division
National Geographic Society
Washington, D.C.

Credits

National Geographic's Driving Guides To America Canada

By Katherine Ashenburg, Alison Kahn, Jeremy Schmidt, and Thomas Schmidt
Photographed by Michael Lewis, Pierre St. Jacques, and others

Published by
The National Geographic Society

Reg Murphy
President and Chief Executive Officer
Gilbert M. Grosvenor
Chairman of the Board
Nina D. Hoffman
Senior Vice President

Prepared by The Book Division

William R. Gray
Vice President and Director
Charles Kogod
Assistant Director
Barbara A. Payne
Editorial Director

Driving Guides to America

Elizabeth L. Newhouse
Director of Travel Books and Series Editor
Cinda Rose
Art Director
Thomas B. Powell III
Illustrations Editor
Caroline Hickey, Barbara A. Noe
Senior Researchers
Carl Mehler
Map Editor and Designer

Staff for this book

Caroline Hickey
Project Manager
Mary Luders
Text Editor
Joan Wolbier
Designer
Thomas B. Powell III
Illustrations Editor

Sean M. Groom
Karin Hayes
Michael H. Higgins
Keith R. Moore
Researchers

Barbara A. Noe
Contributing Editor

Lise S. Sajewski
Copy Editor

Sven M. Dolling, Jill Storm
Map Research
Sven M. Dolling
Map Production
Tibor G. Tóth
Map Relief

Meredith C. Wilcox
Illustrations Assistant
Richard S. Wain
Production Project Manager
Lewis R. Bassford, Lyle Rosbotham
Production

Rhonda J. Brown, Kevin G. Craig, Dale M. Herring, Peggy J. Purdy
Staff Assistants

Elisabeth MacRae-Bobynskyj
Indexer

Daniel M. Nonte, Shana E. Vickers
Contributors

Manufacturing and Quality Management

George V. White, *Director*
John T. Dunn, *Associate Director*
Vincent P. Ryan, *Manager*

Mennonite farmer, St. Jacobs area, Ontario

Cover: Peyton Lake, Banff National Park, Alberta
Raymond Gehman

Previous pages: Spanish Aerocar over Niagara Falls Gorge, Ontario

Facing page: Dawn at Maligne Lake, Jasper National Park, Alberta
Raymond Gehman

Library of Congress CIP data: page 160

Contents

ALASKA
U.S.
CANADA
YUKON TERRITORY
Gold Country
Whitehorse
Haines
ARCTIC CIRCLE
NORTHWEST TERRITORIES
Yellowknife
CANADA
BRITISH COLUMBIA
ALBERTA
Sea to Mountains
Parks Circle
Edmonton
Kamloops
Vancouver
Victoria
WASH.
Calgary
SASKATCHEWAN
Saskatoon North
Saskatoon
MANITOBA
Yoho to Kootenay
IDAHO
Calgary and Dinosaurs
MONT.
Regina
Regina Ramble
Brandon
N.DAK.
Winnipeg Circle
Parks and Prairies
See Great Lakes Guide
Duluth

National parkland
0 400 mi
0 600 km
DSON BAY
NEWFOUNDLAND
LABRADOR
QUEBEC
ONTARIO
SHIELD
Avalon - Bonavista Peninsulas
St. John's
West Coast
Gulf of St. Lawrence
Channel-Port aux Basques
Gaspé Peninsula
Mont-Joli
The Island
P.E.I.
North Sydney
Cape Breton
Charlottetown
Fundy to Kouchibouguac
St. Lawrence Circuit
Quebec
Fredericton
NOVA SCOTIA
Halifax
Montreal Area
Montreal
MAINE
The Saints
Halifax Circle
CAN. U.S.
VT.
N.H.
NEW BRUNSWICK
Ottawa
Capital Region
Lake Huron
MICH.
Toronto
Lake Ontario
NEW YORK
Detroit
Toronto - London Loop
Lake Erie
See Great Lakes Guide

The True North

Moose, Elk Island National Park, Alberta

First impressions can be strangely persevering. When I was a child in upstate New York in the 1950s, "Canada" was a collective noun that embraced the Mounties, hockey, and winter. Now that I have lived in Canada for almost 30 years, my sense of the country is more subtle and more grounded. But something of my childish perception of Canada as romantic and "other" remains and is reinforced when I travel this curious, fascinating, varied, stubborn, reticent country.

Canada is particularly intriguing for Americans as it represents the path we did not take. English Canada's legal system, language, food, and architecture are more than familiar: They are the inheritance of our common Mother Country. But underneath the similarities is something profoundly different that makes Canada what it is—a conservative, loyal connection to England and the other Commonwealth countries. It is relevant to realize that the importance Americans reserve for "life, liberty and the pursuit of happiness" is given by Canadians in the British North America Act to "peace, order and good government."

The other great fact in Canada is, of course, the 20 percent of the population who are French speaking. For Canadians this has meant a history of compromise and tactful cohabitation that occasionally threatens to end in divorce. For the traveler it means something much less fraught—a foreignness that is delightfully, bewilderingly at home in North America. It's a foreignness that extends to time as well as place: Sometimes in the Acadian settlements of New Brunswick, the old town in Quebec City, the villages on the St. Lawrence River's south shore, it can be hard to believe you're in the 20th century.

As for nature, even Canada, the most unboastful of nations, brags about its Rocky Mountains, the sea and mountainscape of Vancouver, the rocky poetry of the Gaspé region, the endless sky of the Prairies. For Americans, the Canadian regions will be reminiscent of the lands to the south—but often less traveled, a bit wilder, a bit more spectacular. And the natives aren't just friendly: Their politeness is legendary. Welcome to the True North.

KATHERINE ASHENBURG

Entering Canada

Citizens and permanent residents of the United States do not need passports or visas to be admitted to Canada, and can usually cross the border without difficulty or delay. However, to speed the process, U.S. citizens should carry some form of identification with evidence of citizenship, such as a passport, a certificate of naturalization, or a voter registration card with a photo ID; permanent residents are advised to bring their residency cards. Parents should carry identification for their children similar to the above. *For answers to other questions, contact your local Canadian consulate or the Canadian Embassy in Washington, D.C.*

About the Guides

NATIONAL GEOGRAPHIC'S DRIVING GUIDES TO AMERICA invite you on memorable road trips through the United States and Canada. Intended both as travel planners and companions, each volume guides you on preplanned tours over a wide variety of terrain to the best places to see and things to do. The authors, expert regional travel writers, star-rate (from none to two ★★) the drives and points of interest to make sure you don't miss their favorites.

All distances and drive times are approximate (if you linger, as you should, plan on considerably more time). Recommended seasons are the best times to go, but roads and sites are open all year unless otherwise noted. Besides the stated days of operation, many sites close on national holidays. For the most up-to-date site information, it's best to call ahead when possible.

Then, with this book and a road map, set off on your adventure through this awesomely beautiful land.

Peggys Cove, Nova Scotia

MAP KEY and ABBREVIATIONS

National Park — NAT. PARK.
National Park Reserve
National Park and Preserve — NAT. PARK RES.
National Recreation Area

National Forest

National Wildlife Area
Provincial Wildlife Reserve

Wilderness Provincial Park
Wilderness Reserve
Provincial Park — PROV. PARK
Nature Park
Local Park

ADDITIONAL ABBREVIATIONS

HIST.	*Historical*
HWY.	*Highway*
Mt.-s.	*Mount, Mountain-s*
NAT.	*National*
N.H.P.	*National Historical Park*
N.H.S.	*National Historic Site*
Pk.	*Park*
PKWY.	*Parkway*
PROV.	*Provincial*
Pt.	*Point*
Rec.	*Recreation*
St.-e.	*Saint-e*

POPULATION

● **Montreal**	500,000 and over
● Laval	50,000 to under 500,000
● Kensington	under 50,000

Featured Drive
Trans-Canada Highway 17
Principal Highway 43 MAJOR MINOR
Secondary Road 11
U.S. Interstate 87
U.S. Federal Highway 95
State Road 31
Trail
Political Border
Ferry FEATURED OTHER
Canal
Continental Divide
Nat. Park Boundary

■ Point of Interest
National Capital
Provincial Capital
+ Elevation, Peak
= Falls
)(Pass

Avalon-Bonavista Peninsulas

● 480 miles/775 km ● 6 days ● Late June to mid-October ● To get here, take the 14-hour ferry to Argentia from North Sydney, Nova Scotia. If you're traveling across the island from the west coast, you can do this drive in reverse, then return via Argentia (Marine Atlantic: 800-341-7981. Fare. Ferry reservations essential, especially in July and August).

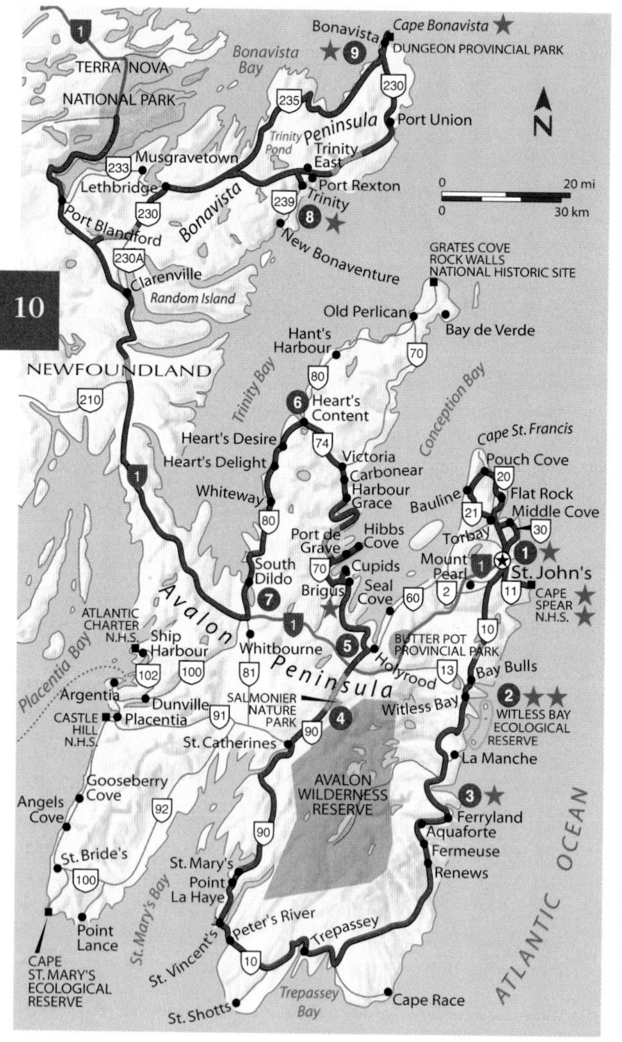

This drive takes you from the storied, salty provincial capital of St. John's—which calls itself North America's oldest city founded by Europeans—"around the bay" (specifically the Avalon and Bonavista Peninsulas). Here, along with startlingly beautiful and varied land- and seascapes, roaming caribou, and the odd roadside moose, are quaint fishing outports where haphazard clusters of saltbox houses cling like barnacles to harborside rock—where the heart and soul of Irish Newfoundland thrives. Here, too, await some major historical sites, including Lord Baltimore's original settlement, John Cabot's credited landfall, and the hill where Marconi received the first transatlantic wireless transmission.

Beginning some 400 million years ago, through the process of plate tectonics, part of the European continent separated and eventually joined the hunk of ancient rock that comprises the island of Newfoundland. This piece—the Avalon Peninsula—dangles like a ragged *H* off the island's southeast corner. At its far eastern edge, facing the North Atlantic, sprawls ❶ **St. John's**★ *(Visitor Center in Confederation Bldg., Prince Philip Dr. 709-729-2830 or 800-563-6353. Guided and self-guided walking tours available).*

On the map since the 1500s, its main draws a perfect harbor and an ocean full of cod, St. John's character has been shaped by the likes of European explorers and fishermen, soldiers and sailors, pirates, misfits, and just plain adventurers. The city still has that offbeat, can't-pin-it-down attitude typical of places at the edge. Despite high unemployment, especially since a 1992 moratorium shut down the cod fishery, St. John's hasn't lost its creative nerve. The arts—dance, music, fine art, crafts, theater, literature—are still prolifically made and played here.

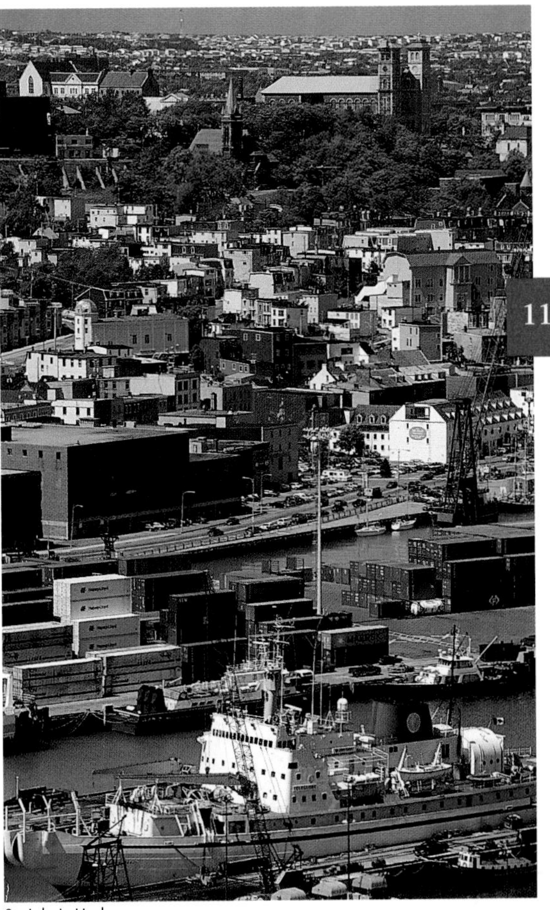
St. John's Harbor

The city starts at the harbor, and you should, too; it's all uphill from there. Explore its colorful streets and steep alleys on foot. You'll go home with tighter calves and a better knowledge of architecture, from plain-faced row houses to fussy Victorians built by merchants and sea captains.

On and off Water and Duckworth Streets, you'll find an array of restaurants, bars, shops, galleries, and businesses. For nightlife, George Street is the place, especially, but not exclusively, for the young and the restless. For a look at contemporary Canadian art, wander through the **Eastern Edge Gallery** *(Harbour Dr. at Clift's-Baird's Cove.*

709-739-1882. Closed Mon.), an artist-run art center. Then go back in time at the **Newfoundland Museum** *(285 Duckworth St. 709-729-2329),* which presents the province's natural and cultural history. The 1855 Romanesque **Basilica of St. John the Baptist** *(200 Military Rd.)* keeps watch over the Narrows. A national historic site, this magnificent stone church features 66 stained-glass windows, an ornate Italianate ceiling, and the haunting "Redeemer in Death" by Irish sculptor John Hogan. Sequestered uphill is the Georgian-style **Commissariat House** *(King's Bridge Rd. 709-729-6730. Mid-June–mid-Oct.),* historic residence and office of the assistant commissary general, restored to its 1830 vintage. Finally stop by **Devon House Craft Gallery** *(59 Duckworth St. 709-753-2749)* to see unusual juried shows.

Canada's second largest national historic site, **Signal Hill★★** was long used to signal the arrival of ships (fortifications date from the Napoleonic Wars). Here, in 1762, France lost to England the final battle of the Seven Years' War in North America. A performance of 19th-century military drills, known as the Signal Hill Tattoo *(twice daily Wed.-Thurs., and Sat.-Sun. mid-July–mid-Aug.; adm. fee),* is reenacted by members of the Royal Newfoundland Companies. Crowning the hill near the site where Guglielmo Marconi received the first transatlantic wireless message in 1901, 1897 **Cabot Tower** honors the 400th anniversary of the island's discovery by John Cabot and Queen Victoria's Diamond Jubilee. It's all presented audiovisually at the **Interpretation Centre** *(709-772-5367. Closed Sat.-Sun. mid-Oct.–mid-July; adm. fee).* The views from the Lookout, as Signal Hill was originally known, are unmatched. On a clear day you can see Newfoundland's oldest existing lighthouse (1835), now restored as a museum at spectacular **Cape Spear National Historic Site★★** *(Hwy. 11. 709-772-5367. Lighthouse tours mid-June–Labor Day; adm. fee),* Canada's eastern-

Basilica of St. John the Baptist, St. John's

most point. It's a great place to watch the sunrise, and you see it before anyone else in the country.

Walk down to the old village of **Quidi Vidi★★** (KID-dy VID-dy), since 1826 site of the festive Royal St. John's Regatta *(first Wed. in Aug.)*. The 3,075-acre area includes the campus of the Memorial University of Newfoundland and the **Art Gallery of Newfoundland and Labrador★** *(Arts and Culture Centre, Allandale Rd. and Prince Philip Pkwy. 709-737-8209. Closed Mon.)*, exhibiting fine art and crafts by primarily provincial artists.

Cape Spear lighthouse

Don't miss the **Fluvarium★★** *(Nagle's Pl. off Allandale Rd. 709-754-3474. Closed Mon.-Fri. Jan.-March; adm. fee)*, featuring nine underwater windows that look into Nagle's Hill Brook, plus imaginative exhibits on freshwater ecology, issues, and uses. Then tour the **Fisheries and Marine Institute of Memorial University★** *(155 Ridge Rd. 709-778-0200. Tours mid-June–Aug. Mon.-Fri., by appt. rest of year)* to see the world's largest flume tank and a full-size ship bridge and navigational simulator. The **Institute for Marine Dynamics★** *(Kerwin Pl. 709-772-0029. Tours July-Aug. Mon.-Fri.)* contains the world's longest ice tank, a giant towing tank, and a model ocean. **Memorial University Botanical Gardens★** *(306 Mount Scio Rd. 709-737-8590. Daily July-Aug., Wed.-Sun. May-June and Sept.-Nov.; adm. fee)* exhibits native and cultivated plants in a variety of formal gardens and natural habitats linked by trails.

There are few cities where the wild is so exhilaratingly present and accessible as St. John's. Wander the expanding trail network, to old favorites Signal Hill and the colorful Battery village, and above Quidi Vidi, where you can pick berries and be alone with sea, sky, wind, and gulls.

Slip out of town for a scenic, 40-odd-mile (60-km) side trip around **Marine Drive★★,** north of St. John's *(from Logy Bay Rd./Hwy. 30 to Marine Dr.)*. Visit Memorial University's **Ocean Sciences Centre★** *(Logy Bay. 709-737-3706. Tours daily mid-May–mid-Sept. and Sun. April–mid-May and mid-Sept.–Nov.; adm. fee)*. The oceanside marine research lab resembles a spaceship more than the sea anemone it was designed to function like, circulating seawater from Logy Bay through the facility. Tour the observation tanks

Ocean Sciences Centre, Logy Bay

and oceanographic equipment, where exhibits interpret research in aquaculture, ecology, and seal behavior (observe the seals for yourself out back).

Marine Drive sweeps up and around the bluffs, above clear-water coves, through small communities, some more charming than others. At **Middle Cove,** walk down to the cobble beach where, in mid-June, hordes of silver, smelt-like capelin run with the tide to spawn on the rocks. You may even see an iceberg.

Detour from Hwy. 20 down to **Flat Rock,** so named for the rocky ledge angling from the water. At **Flat Rock Grotto,** the largest religious grotto east of Montreal, the Stations of the Cross are built dramatically into the rock facing the sea. From **Pouch Cove,** one of the island's earliest settlements, loop back on Hwy. 21, ducking down to the pretty village of **Bauline,** to Hwy. 20 at Torbay, and return to town.

From St. John's, head down the southern shore on Pitts Memorial Drive and Hwy. 10 south. Several outfits run boat tours from Bay Bulls and surrounding communities to ❷ **Witless Bay Ecological Reserve★★** *(Visitor Center Hwy. 10, Witless Bay. 709-432-3200. Mid-June–Labor Day).* Comprised of four small islands and surrounding waters, this is the summer breeding ground of more than two million seabirds, including petrels, Atlantic puffins, kittiwakes, murres, razorbills, fulmars, black-backed gulls, and guillemots. While you're guaranteed a feast of bird-watching, chances are you'll see whales and porpoises, too.

Seal, Ocean Sciences Centre, Logy Bay

The route skirts the 335-square-mile Avalon Wilderness Reserve, passing fishing villages settled centuries ago by Welsh, English, and then Irish fishermen and farmers, whose legacies predominate in the names, faces, and pure Irish accents you hear around these parts.

Pull off at ❸ **Ferryland★,** where in 1621 the first Lord Baltimore established one of England's earliest settlements in Canada. Have a look at **Ferryland Community Museum** *(Off Hwy. 10. 709-432-2711)* and the old stone

Holy Trinity Church *(Hwy. 10)*. Today Ferryland is the site of an exciting archaeological project so accessible you can look over the archaeologists' shoulders. History and artifacts are exhibited at the **Colony of Avalon Interpretation Centre**★★ *(709-432-3200. Mid-June–mid-Oct.; adm. fee)*; you can also see the artifacts being processed at the on-site laboratory. Stroll from here to the old lighthouse—for the full effect, walk out across the famous downs, or barrens.

From here on the vistas get bigger, the landscape more barren and rugged and, well, more *northern*. The sense of being swallowed by the sheer vastness intensifies as you round the peninsula. (Unfortunately, you may also be swallowed by fog along this vulnerable stretch of coast.) Watch for caribou (some of the world's largest), especially between Trepassey and Peter's River. In summer, they migrate down here from the interior wilderness to escape the heat and voracious black flies.

Middle Cove Beach Provincial Park

Beyond **St. Vincent's,** a whale-watching spot, follow Hwy. 90 through the Irish community of ❹ **St. Mary's** toward Trans-Canada 1. About 7 miles (11 km) south of Trans-Canada 1, **Salmonier Nature Park** *(Hwy. 90. 709-229-7888. June–mid-Oct.)* features native animals and plants and nature trails on almost 3,000 diverse acres. Pick up the next leg of the main drive at ❺ **Holyrood.** Here the road wraps around picturesque coves, wends by a bevy of fishing villages, rolls along rocky ridges, lending long views that make your breath catch.

Head north into the heart of enchanting **Brigus**★. The village's circular plan and Protestant churches reflect its English heritage, dating from the early 1600s. Once a major sealing port and home to many sea captains,

Brigus's favorite son is Arctic explorer Capt. Robert Bartlett, who delivered Adm. Robert Peary to the North Pole in 1909. A self-guided walking tour *(maps available)* highlights **Ye Olde Stone Barn Museum★** *(4 Magistrate's Hill. 709-528-3298. Daily mid-June–Labor Day, Sat.-Sun. Labor Day–mid-Oct.; adm. fee),* showcasing Brigus and Bartlett family history, plus priceless newsreels featuring "Captain Bob" himself. Also visit **Hawthorne Cottage★** *(South St. 709-753-9262. Mid-May–mid-Oct.; adm. fee)* and tour Bartlett's picturesque house and garden.

In 1610 English merchant-adventurer John Guy established a plantation at neighboring **Cupids** (originally Cuper's Cove), the first English colony in Canada. Excavation of the site began in 1995; tours of the archaeological dig are arranged at the **Cupids Museum** *(Seaforest Dr. 709-528-3500. Mid-June–mid-Sept.).*

Proceed north on Hwy. 70, detouring out the Port de Grave Peninsula to **Hibbs Cove.** Among the flotsam and jetsam displayed at the small **Fisherman's Museum** *(709-786-3900. Late June–Labor Day, by appt. rest of year; adm. fee)* are such items as a bed rock, a dead box, a lassie keg, a flat-assed kettle, piss quicks, and vintage photographs—a poignant monument for posterity to Newfoundland's fishermen and traditional outport life. Farther up the coast, at **Harbour Grace,** you're greeted by the great rusting hulk

One-room schoolhouse and Porter House, Hibbs Cove

of the S.S. *Kyle,* a coastal steamer beached here in 1962. Amelia Earhart launched her famous transatlantic flight from **Harbour Grace Airstrip** in 1932. Drive down Water Street to the historic district where, on the former site of pirate Peter Easton's fort, the 1870 redbrick Customs Office holds the **Conception Bay Museum** *(Water St. 709-596-5465. June–mid-Sept.),* with exhibits on Earhart, Easton, aviation, fishing, and local and provincial history. Nearby is the venerable **St. Paul's Anglican Church** (1835), Newfoundland's oldest stone church still standing.

To the north, as you enter the crusty old town of **Carbonear,** the **Railway Station Museum** *(Water St. 709-596-2532. June–Labor Day)* contains historical displays, genealogical records, and visitor information about this former commercial center. Take the high road out of Carbonear to Hwy. 74 at Victoria. For the next 9 miles (14.5 km), barrel across one of those lonesome lunar Newfoundlandscapes, wild and beautiful barrens punctuated with stunted spruce and shallow ponds.

Matters of the heart prevail around Trinity Bay's eastern shore. At ❻ **Heart's Content,** visit the **Heart's Content Cable Station★** *(Hwy. 80. 709-583-2160. Mid-June–mid-Oct.),* the western terminal of the first successful transatlantic communications cable laid in 1866 from Valentia, Ireland, to the beach here (you can still see the cable entry). The historic station, in operation from 1875 to 1965, now exhibits the original bells, whistles, and other equipment, with interpretive displays.

Drive south on Hwy. 80, through Heart's Desire and Heart's Delight. As you come through **Whiteway,** look for the striking, "three-masted" rock floating in the bay like some sculptor's vision of a sailing fleet, all the more dramatic when backlit by the late sun.

In ❼ **South Dildo,** a great wooden whale breaches beside the roadside **Whaling and Sealing Museum** *(709-582-2317. Late June–Labor Day; adm. fee),* dedicated to two of the area's former economic mainstays, with displays of Beothuk Indian artifacts.

It's about 5 miles (8 km) from here to Trans-Canada 1. Drive northwest across the rock-strewn tundra of the isthmus and past Clarenville to Hwy. 230, which leads up the Bonavista Peninsula. Beautiful Trinity Pond signals the upcoming turnoff for ❽ **Trinity★,** a gem not to be missed. Picture the ideal of an outport and this place embodies it—like a stage set, almost too perfect to be real. Settled in 1501, it became a prosperous and progressive English fishing and mercantile town, now preserved as a national heritage community. At the

Relatively Speaking

Douse the killick. Fish'n'brewis. Loodle-laddle. Spannytickle. Slieveen. Grog bit. Glutch. If you sometimes get the feeling they're speaking a foreign language here, that's because they are—at least in part. With strains of West Country English planted by fishermen in the early 1700s; Anglo-Irish, brought from southeastern Ireland by laborers and immigrants during the 18th and 19th centuries; and, of course, words invented right here, Newfoundlandese is so distinctive and regional, there's an entire dictionary devoted to it.

Trinity Interpretation Centre *(West St. 709-464-2042. Mid-June–mid-Oct.; guided and self-guided tours available)*, shore up on local history and visitor information, then ditch the car; Trinity's narrow lanes and historic sites should be explored on foot. **Trinity Museum and Archives** *(Church Rd. 709-464-3720. Mid-June–mid-Sept.; adm. fee)* is bursting at the beams with more than 2,000 artifacts, old photos, and historic records.

Other highlights include the Hiscock House, Lester-Garland Premises, and the Green Family Forge–Blacksmith Museum. If your schedule allows, take in the perennial favorite of the area's exceptional summer theater festival, the Trinity Pageant *(Rising Tide Theatre. 709-738-3256. Call for schedule; adm. fee)*, a moveable theatrical feast dramatizing events from Newfoundland history, performed all around the town.

Back on the main road, continue around Trinity Bight, the rugged, indented coast between Bonaventure Head and Horse Chops. The ocean is close now; you can smell it and feel its chill bite. Beyond Port Rexton and Trinity East, senses reel at the boundless, pond-pocked barrens.

Swing along Hwy. 230 through unique **Port Union.** This was built as a model town by Sir William Coaker and his 1908 Fishermen's Protective Union, a group that quickly became one of Newfoundland's first cooperatives—the Fisherman's Union Trading Company.

Just before reaching 9 **Bonavista**★ *(Visitor Center at Town Hall, Church St. 709-468-7816. Mon.-Fri.)* the road crests, offering a fabulous overlook on this 500-year-old seaport sprawled hither and thither across the treeless barrens at the peninsula's tip, its buildings like little toy houses, dropped every which way.

The town was not designed for cars; leave yours by some discernible landmark, then lose yourself in the labyrinth of narrow, often unmarked, lanes and old wooden buildings. Everything is old here, but several historic sites stand out: **Ryan Premises National Historic Site**★ *(Ryan's Hill. 709-722-5364. Late June–late Oct.; adm. fee)*, a newly restored complex, is dedicated to the story of the East Coast Fishery and contains the **Bonavista Museum** *(709-468-2880)*, a repository of community artifacts and history. The nearby **Mockbeggar Property** *(Mockbeggar Rd. 709-729-2460. Mid-June–mid-Oct.)* preserves the fine house-museum of Senator F. Gordon Bradley.

For the Birds

For an up-close and unforgettable look at some 60,000 nesting seabirds, head down to **Cape St. Mary's Ecological Reserve** *(Hwy. 100)*. The steep, 328-plus-foot-tall cliffs, like avian condos, offer a range of accommodations that suit the needs of summering kittiwakes, cormorants, murres, razorbills, guillemots, gulls, and the fourth largest gannet colony in North America. As a bonus, pods of humpback, fin, and minke whales pass between July and August. There are also an interpretive center and a 0.6-mile (1-km) cliff walk to view Bird Rock, a 300-foot sea stack teeming with gannets.

Terra Nova National Park

Next, take the gorgeous shore road out to **Cape Bonavista★,** the reputed, not to say disputed, 1497 landfall of John Cabot (also a prime whale-watching spot). Crowning the point at land's end is Bonavista's signature, the candy-striped lighthouse (1843) and keeper's quarters, restored to 1870 vintage. Exhibits in the adjacent **Interpretive Center** *(709-468-7444. Mid-June–mid-Oct.)* showcase lighthouse technology and the life and work of lightkeepers, and a statue of Cabot commands the bluff. Then stop by nearby **Dungeon Provincial Park,** where the forces of erosion have worn a great, gaping hole and two arched sea gates in the sedimentary rock.

Next, meander along Hwy. 235 down the rocky coast of Bonavista Bay through a succession of long-settled fishing outports to the junction with Trans-Canada 1. As a side trip, drive west on Trans-Canada 1 to **Terra Nova National Park** *(709-533-2801. Call for hours; adm. fee).* This wild and diverse 154-square-mile preserve of boreal forest, barrens, bogs, and coastline shelters moose, lynx, black bears, eagles, ospreys, and whales. Along with nature trails and lookouts, explore the park's new Marine Interpretive Centre's exhibits and aquariums.

Return to St. John's or Argentia; if you're leaving from Channel-Port aux Basques, continue on Trans-Canada 1.

West Coast★

● 620 miles/1,000 km one way ● 5 days ● Mid-June to mid-October ● To get here, take the 6-hour ferry to Channel-Port aux Basques from North Sydney, Nova Scotia (Marine Atlantic: 902-794-5814 or 800-341-7981. Fare; reservations recommended).

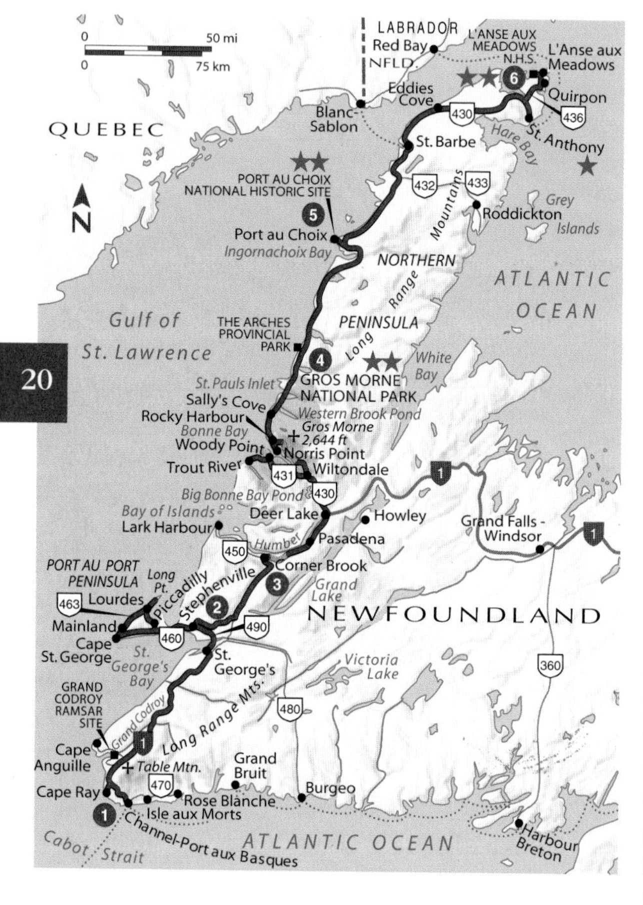

They call it the Rock, this island portion of Canada's tenth province, Newfoundland and Labrador. It takes work to get here—but that's part of the adventure, really. There's nothing like pulling into a new port, especially in the early morning mist, to rouse your inner explorer.

This long, linear drive up the island's rugged and remote west coast, from Channel-Port aux Basques to the tip of the Great Northern Peninsula, rewards with a wealth of natural and historic wonders. A place of staggering elemental beauty, here you find ancient mountains and fjords, cliffs and crashing sea, beaches, forest, and windswept barrens, and a panoply of wildlife—moose, caribou, black bears, bald eagles, whales—plus weathered fishing villages. While the west coast's geological history is as old as earth, its human story goes back some 9,000 years, from prehistoric cultures and Viking explorers, to French, Basque, Scottish, and English settlers. The highlights are two UNESCO world heritage sites: spectacular Gros Morne National Park, with some of the planet's oldest rocks; and L'Anse aux Meadows National Historic

Site, the first known Viking settlement in the New World.

There's no particular reason to linger in the ferry terminus of ❶ **Channel-Port aux Basques,** where this drive begins, other than to scare up breakfast if you've overnighted on the boat. You'll go north on Trans-Canada 1—but before you leave the area, consider taking a side trip *(60 mi/95 km round-trip on Hwy. 470 E)* along the rugged southern coastal plain to the beautiful, old fishing village of **Rose Blanche.** Newfoundland boasts extraordinary landscapes, and this is one not to be missed. The empty rockbound and heath-covered expanse stretches end-

Channel-Port aux Basques

lessly. Even the larger settlements seem blips in this big primeval scene. As the road climbs, you get some jaw-dropping views. Hike out on the "Neck" to see the ruins of the 1873 granite lighthouse. (Consider life here *before* the road came through in 1960: "The year," as one woman measured it, "before Grandmother died." Many south-coast communities are still accessible only by boat.)

Backtrack to Trans-Canada 1, the single road across the island. (Road crews worked from both ends to meet in the middle, as planned: "We'll finish the drive in '65.") You're soon in sight of the stark, often fog-shrouded Long Range Mountains, part of the ancient Appalachian chain.

High-wind warnings allude to the mercurial presence of 1,699-foot **Table Mountain,** an anomalous formation that generates its own weather patterns. Summit gusts have been known to exceed 99 miles per hour, strong enough to derail trains.

Old locomotive, Corner Brook

Beyond here the rock yields briefly to the green and fertile **Codroy Valley,** the island's richest agricultural region, where tractors supplant lobster traps. Descendants of early Scottish settlers still farm here. Tucked between the Anguille and Long Range Mountains, the valley shelters the island's only wetlands, the internationally recognized **Grand Codroy Ramsar Site.**

The landscape changes again as you drive northeast across the wide valley of the Grand Codroy River. The mountains dwindle to low, spruce-clad hills that gradually flatten as the dense forest turns scruffy and stunted, battered by prevailing southwest winds.

Detour west on Hwy. 490 to the former American Air Force Base of ❷ **Stephenville,** now a service-industrial center and host to an annual music and theater festival in midsummer. It's also gateway to the beautiful **Port au Port Peninsula,** the French heartland of Terre Neuve. Nicknamed the French Shore, it was settled by Acadians in the 18th and 19th centuries; isolation has preserved their language and culture.

To make the 85-mile (135-km) scenic loop around the peninsula, cross the causeway onto the peninsula and begin a roller-coaster ride along the coastal bluffs. (What look like colorful outhouses along the roadside are actually bus stops.) Stay close to the water and follow Hwy. 463 toward Piccadilly, around the bay to Lourdes. Detour out to spectacular **Long Point,** then turn southwest down the rugged gulf coast to the **Mainland** (la Grande Terre), where the new highway leads up through great portals of blasted rock. The trees dwindle, shrink, then disappear, and before you know it, you're in a barren landscape reminiscent of the Arctic.

Descend to **Cape St. George,** heart of Newfoundland's Acadian country, where bay meets gulf, and you're soon back in that greener realm. If it's August, take in the annual French folk festival, Une Longue Veillée ("a long night"). As you cross the broad plain back to Trans-

Canada 1 on Hwy. 460, notice the bonsai-like trees, their aspect permanently disfigured by prevailing winter winds.

It's a pretty stretch from here to ❸ **Corner Brook** *(Visitor Center 709-639-9792).* You will see more frequent signs of the pulp-and-paper industry, which dominates the economy of the island's interior. From its center at the mouth of the lovely, salmon-rich Humber River, Corner Brook climbs into the surrounding hills. A rail hub and timber town, the city grew up around the pulp-and-paper company, one of the world's largest, which has been chuffing away by the river since 1925. In town, the **Art Gallery** *(Arts and Culture Centre, University Dr. 709-637-2582)* features the work of Newfoundland artists. The **Railway Museum** *(Station Rd. 709-634-6089. June-Aug.)* displays historic, narrow-gauge rolling stock, including the last surviving steam locomotive and a snowplow train. A national historic site and spectacular lookout, the **Captain James Cook Monument** *(Atlantic Ave. to Crow Hill Rd.)* honors the British explorer who charted this area in 1767. A side trip *(about 60 mi/100 km round-trip)* along the historic **Captain Cook Trail** *(Hwy. 450)* traces the Humber Arm out to the magnificent Bay of Islands.

Travel northeast along Trans-Canada 1 through the Humber Valley, which produces some 80 percent of Newfoundland's strawberries. About 30 miles (48 km) along,

Tablelands, Gros Morne National Park

Trout River fishing village, Gros Morne National Park

you reach **Deer Lake,** the gateway to the **Great Northern Peninsula** and the **Viking Trail** (Hwy. 430).

Proceed north on Hwy. 430 a few miles past the resort area of **Big Bonne Bay Pond** (Newfoundlanders call almost any freshwater body a "pond," regardless of its size), to wild and beautiful ❹ **Gros Morne National Park**★★ *(Visitor Center off Hwy. 430, Rocky Harbour. 709-458-2066. Adm. fee),* covering nearly 700 square miles. Gros Morne's appeal is elemental. Plainly speaking, it's the rocks that make this place, nicknamed the Galápagos of Geology, so special. In 1987 the park was named a UNESCO world heritage site, mainly for its rare and revealing bedrock that supports the geological theory of plate tectonics, but also for its flora and fauna, fossils, coast, dunes, fjords, bogs, mountains, and a human history going back 5,000 years.

At Wiltondale, head west on Hwy. 431 to tour the park's spectacular southern section, containing its most significant geological feature: the **Tablelands,** a rare, prime example of the earth's mantle. After a steep ascent, tundra-topped Gros Morne Mountain—roughly translated as "big isolated hill," with a nuance of "gloomy"—lies dead ahead like a giant loaf. Swing up the bay toward the bare, flat-topped Tablelands, an anomaly forced from beneath the ocean some 500 million years ago. If you do only one walk in the park, make it this one: A level path leads from the parking lot at the Tablelands lookout and across this brown, desertlike high plateau, eerily silent except for the wind and the occasional bird call.

Continue west and visit the once isolated fishing outport of **Trout River,** then backtrack to explore the scenic and historic town of **Woody Point** before heading north on Hwy. 430. Stop at **Rocky Harbour,** the park's main community, where the Visitor Center offers interpretive exhibits and an inspiring multi-image presentation. Then turn south, following signs to the quaint communities of **Neddy Harbour** and **Norris Point.** Head back through Rocky Harbour and onto Hwy. 430 to where the 1898 **lighthouse** *(June-Sept.)* at beautiful **Lobster Cove Head** presents an interesting exhibit on local history. Paths lead around the headland and down to the cobble beach.

Of Moose and Men

Surprisingly, the ubiquitous moose is not native to Newfoundland, but was introduced as a supplementary food source and recreation for sportsmen. In 1878 a cow and a bull were imported from Nova Scotia and released at Gander Bay. The apparently reticent couple made a negligible contribution to posterity. Two more pairs, introduced in 1904 and set loose near Deer Lake, were more successful: By the late 1980s, with only one natural predator, the black bear, and no deadly parasites, the population had soared to about 150,000. Despite two open hunting seasons, moose have proliferated.

Almost 5 miles (8 km) north of Sally's Cove, sheer cliffs of billion-year-old granite rise up to 2,000 feet, hiding the entrance to spectacular **Western Brook Pond.** Commonly called an inland fjord, this pure, deep, and cold 10-mile-long lake was carved by glaciers. A 1.8-mile (3-km) interpretive walk leads across the coastal plain to the launch for a fabulous, 2.5-hour narrated cruise *(709-458-2066. Tours June–Sept.; fare)* between the cliffs, past waterfalls and assorted wildlife.

About 2 miles (3 km) up the road, watch for an irresistible white-sand beach. To reach it, turn left at the entrance to Western Brook picnic area; a trail leads over the dunes, down to this gorgeous strand.

Western Brook Pond, Gros Morne National Park

A short distance north, and still within the park, **Broom Point** *(Mid-June–mid-Sept.)* preserves a real-life fishing story. From the 1940s through 1975, the Mudge brothers used the site as their summer fishing premises. Now, retired fishermen are on hand to guide you through the restored fish store and furnished cabin. A short walk leads down to a quiet, little 19th-century cemetery.

Drive across shallow, boulder-strewn St. Paul's Inlet, past beaches that recall driftwood graveyards. A few miles beyond the park limits, **The Arches Provincial Park** harbors an unusual triple-arched limestone formation at the sea's edge, its three windows open on the crashing surf. The beach here is a rock hound's dream.

By now you will have noticed how the land and the vegetation change as you travel up the peninsula. First, trees shrink in size, giving way to alpine krummholz, or

Archaeological dig, L'Anse aux Meadows National Historic Site

tuckamore—elfin forest of stunted, backswept balsam fir and spruce—then vast tracts of barrens along exposed coastal bluffs. Where the road moves inland, the trees return. If you're wondering about those tended plots and motley scarecrows along the road, they're roadside gardens (mostly potatoes, plus other root vegetables), an old Northern Peninsula tradition.

Swing around Ingornachoix Bay, then take a side trip to the windy, working town of **Port au Choix**—the early French settlers' "port of choice" and the fishing capital of western Newfoundland. This marks the southern end of the so-called French Shore, along which France retained inshore fishing rights from 1713 until 1904. Thousands of years before the French arrived, three ancient cultures lived in the area. ❺ **Port au Choix National Historic Site**★★ *(Point Riche. 709-861-3522. Mid-June–mid-Sept.; adm. fee)* preserves and interprets several archaeological sites, including a major Maritime Archaic burial ground and a Dorset Eskimo site, and numerous artifacts.

Continue up the rugged French Shore. The sense of remoteness intensifies as you proceed through a string of isolated fishing villages. At **Eddies Cove,** leave civilization behind and veer east across the peninsula's barren tip. Near St. Anthony airport, the road swings northeast into a more interesting landscape of worn redrock benches, mountains, and rolling hills, toward Pistolet Bay.

Drive north about 18 miles (29 km) on wildly beautiful Hwy. 436, past such oddly named villages as Quirpon (car-POON) and Griquet (CRICK-et). There's no traveler's anonymity on this road less traveled; people here make eye contact right through your windshield. Stop at **L'Anse aux Meadows National Historic Site★★** *(Hwy. 436. 709-623-2608. Mid-June–Sept.; adm. fee),* a UNESCO world heritage site. This is where Norse explorer Leif Eriksson set up a base camp nearly a thousand years ago, the first known European settlement in the New World.

Stop by the Visitor Center to see a fascinating film about the settlement's discovery, as well as audiovisual exhibits on Viking history and culture, then visit the site (*do* take the guided tour, so you know what you're looking at). A boardwalk trail leads to the dig site at land's end. There's enough wildness left in this elemental landscape to let you imagine away the signs of civilization and the centuries. Alongside the actual excavations, full-scale reconstructions of three of the original eight sod structures show you what the settlement looked like, down to the smoky fire in the longhouse. Finally, walk the headland trail.

Next, visit the village of **L'Anse aux Meadows** (a spectacular sunset perch), and before returning stop at **St. Anthony** *(Visitor Center 709-454-2812).* Originally a seasonal fishing station for French and Basque fishermen, St. Anthony is the home of the famous Grenfell Mission, which was founded in 1898 by English missionary Wilfred Grenfell to provide medical services to the isolated communities of northern Newfoundland and Labrador.

Grenfell's former home, now the **Grenfell House Museum★** *(709-454-2281. Mid-May–Oct., by appt. rest of year; adm. fee),* reveals the life and spirit of this remarkable man through family photos, personal memoirs and artwork, books, letters, news clippings, and samples of the regional crafts he promoted. Born as a cottage industry, community-based **Grenfell Handicrafts★** *(Off West St., across from Curtis Hospital. 709-454-3576. Closed Sat.-Sun. Nov.–mid-May)* is still marketing its famous traditional hooked mats, embroidered parkas, knits, and carvings after more than a hundred years. See the magnificent **Jordi Bonet Murals** *(Curtis Hospital rotunda),* eight huge stone panels dedicated to the Grenfell Mission workers and to the people of Newfoundland and Labrador.

For a windblown experience of the environment, head out to **Fishing Point,** a spectacular lookout for icebergs, whales, and seabirds. Then turn around and enjoy it all again with a southbound perspective on the return drive.

Leif's Camp

The remains of eight buildings and many artifacts testify to visits by Norsemen at L'Anse aux Meadows—and tell us that they traveled farther south into Vinland, the rich, temperate land of wild grapes extolled by Leif Eriksson, stretching to the southern shores of the Gulf of St. Lawrence. Here they met, and fought, the many native peoples they called Skraelings. After a few years these hostilities, combined with the difficulties of maintaining an outpost so far from home, caused the Norse to return to Greenland. Although they made sporadic visits to northern regions such as Labrador and Baffin Island, another 500 years would elapse before Europeans were ready to settle North America.

Cape Breton★

● 280 miles/450 km ● 5 days ● Mid-June through September

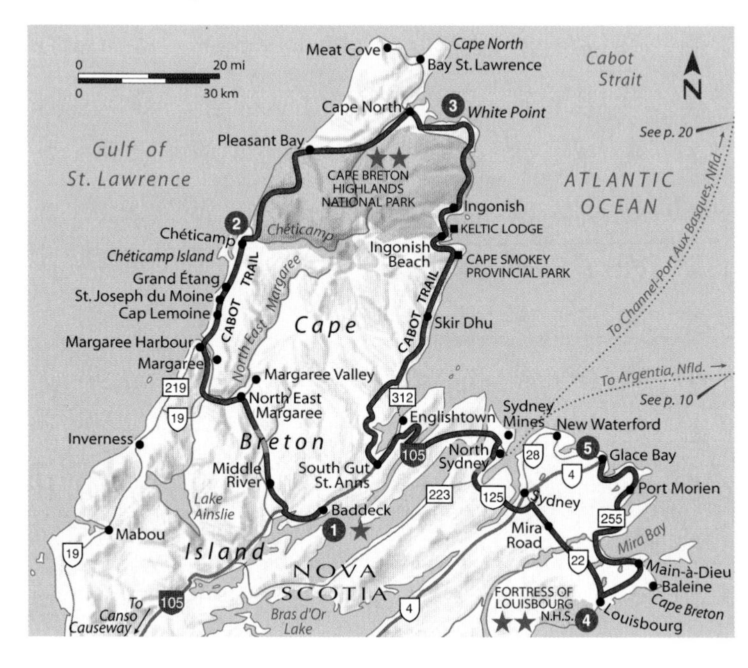

For sheer scenic spectacle, this drive has few rivals in Atlantic Canada, indeed in North America. From Baddeck, Alexander Graham Bell's adopted home, it weaves around the famous Cabot Trail—named for explorer John Cabot—past timeless fishing villages, through Cape Breton Highlands National Park—a wild place of moody highlands, steep headlands plunging dramatically to the sea, regal woodlands, and plentiful wildlife. Here also you find the irrepressible cultural heart of the island, where Scottish and Acadian traditions—music, dance, food, crafts, language—live on. The route then loops around to the incomparable Fortress of Louisbourg National Historic Site, then up the jigsawed Atlantic Coast, where inventor Guglielmo Marconi built his signal towers, to the historic mining town of Glace Bay.

As soon as you cross Canso Causeway, which joins mainland Nova Scotia and Cape Breton Island, you may think you've died and gone to Scotland. Where else but Cape Breton might you find Highland dancers stepping and whooping jubilantly to flying fiddles right along the highway? (The Visitor Center at gateway Port Hastings knows how to put you in the mood.) Follow Trans-Canada 105 to ❶ **Baddeck★** *(Welcome Centre, Chebucto St. 902-295-1911),* where you begin your drive.

Alexander Graham Bell, humanitarian and prolific inventor, chose this pretty village on Bras d'Or Lake as his summer home and laboratory. The **Alexander Graham Bell National Historic Site★★** *(Chebucto St. 902-295-2069. Adm. fee mid-May–mid-Oct.)* presents an exciting, interactive walk through Bell's world, with audiovisual installations, photographs, and the world's most complete collection of his memorabilia, artifacts, and equipment related to communications, aviation, and marine engineering. Don't miss the excellent introductory films.

Baddeck is a fun town to browse, with plenty of shops, galleries, restaurants, and a lively government

Cabot Trail along western coastline of Cape Breton Highlands National Park

wharf. Special events include the Bras d'Or Festival of the Arts *(July–mid-Oct.)* and the Bras d'Or Yacht Club Annual Regatta, held the first full week in August since 1904.

Drive a few miles west on Trans-Canada 105 to join the Cabot Trail. Then head north to North East Margaree through the narrow, wooded valley of the Middle River, a favorite among salmon and trout anglers. After about 20 miles (32 km), stop by the **Margaree Salmon Museum** *(Off the Cabot Trail, North East Margaree. 902-248-2848. Mid-June–mid-Oct.; adm. fee).* Housed in an old schoolhouse, the little museum boasts an impressive collection of flies, rods, and tackle, plus photographs of famous guides.

If you happen to be in the area on the right night, go on down to the **Normaway Inn Barn★** *(Old Egypt Rd., Margaree Valley. 902-248-2987. July-Aug. Wed., June and Sept.-Oct. Fri.; adm. fee)* for the weekly family (no alcohol served) ceilidh—a traditional Celtic "jam." This popular local event is a guaranteed good time and an opportunity to see some mean fiddling and step-dancing by young and old; stick around for the dance afterward.

Sculptor in his studio, Chéticamp

Wind along the river valley to the coast, where place-names—and the popular motif of the tricolored Acadian flag—preserve the legacy of French settlement. As you travel north, the landscape becomes more rugged, more remote and barren, the communities become smaller and more scattered. You can't miss **Joe's Garden of Scarecrows** in Cap Lemoine. The curious group of about 110 masked characters grew from a few figures in Joe Delaney's garden. "Now we have no vegetables," says his daughter, Ethel, who runs the adjacent take-out and gift shop, "but a garden of scarecrows."

Up the hill in St. Joseph du Moine, stop by the kooky and colorful **Gallery La Bella Mona Lisa** *(Cabot Trail. 902-224-2560)*, a gallery of provincial folk art. The artist-owner displays his own whimsical work.

At ❷ **Chéticamp,** gateway to the highlands, the landmark **St. Peter's Church** (1893) was built of stone from Chéticamp Island, hauled over the ice by parishioners. The small **Acadian Museum** *(774 Main St. 902-224-2170. Mid-May–Oct.; donation)* features vintage hooked rugs, the local cottage industry, and settlers' artifacts, with demonstrations by craftspeople. See the exquisitely detailed works in wool by internationally acclaimed rug hooker Elizabeth LeFort, a Chéticamp native, plus an eclectic collection of antiques and odds and ends at **Les Trois Pignons** *(902-224-2612. Daily July-Aug., Mon.-Fri. May-June and Sept.-Oct.; adm. fee).*

The moody highlands loom ahead at the entrance to **Cape Breton Highlands National Park★★** *(Park Information Centres at Chéticamp and Ingonish Beach. 902-224-2306. Adm. fee),* the rugged roof of Nova Scotia. The rock here shares a common geological history with that of the Scottish Highlands. The Chéticamp information center provides a useful introduction to the park's natural history, with exhibits and a slide show. To take advantage of pull-offs, detours, and serendipitous diversions, allow at least five hours for this 66-mile (106-km) park drive.

Just beyond the parking lot, the towering walls of **Chéticamp Canyon**—typical of the narrow, steep-walled ravines dissecting the highland plateau—close in. Everywhere along the coast you see evidence of the powerful forces of erosion. The roller-coaster road offers views so overwhelming, so big and so grand, that you don't know where to look first. (Look ahead at the road, though, snaking through the rock mountains and you'll believe in the miracles of engineering.) Watch for whales and bald eagles and monitor the mood of the mountains; it changes as constantly as the weather.

The road ascends surely and steadily, skirting dizzingly steep chasms, and past a kaleidoscope of environments—lakes, bogs, forest. The scent of wood fires drifts from campgrounds, mingling with the fragrance of boreal black spruce. Beyond the spectacular **MacKenzie Mountain** look-off, veer from the gulf coast toward the Atlantic. The drive twists and turns steeply up **North Mountain** to an ear-popping altitude of 1,499 feet (if you're chugging on four cylinders, this climb will slow you down considerably). At the top, you may see moose foraging by the roadside, particularly in early evening.

The Atlantic side is kinder and gentler than the gulf. Here, low headlands, sheltered coves, and fishing villages replace the jagged, worn cliffs and empty, narrow beaches.

Bay St. Lawrence, north of Cape Breton Highlands National Park

Costumed interpreters, Fortress of Louisbourg National Historic Site

Take a scenic detour around the headland at ❸ **White Point.** The route promises a feast of gorgeous views, seductive hideaways, and tranquil fishing villages before swinging back to the main road.

Drive on to the **Ingonish** area, defined by two beautiful bays. The historic, Tudor-style **Keltic Lodge** *(902-285-2880)* commands the cliffs of Middle Head, above the sandy crescent at Ingonish Beach. Walk the easy trail from the beach to Freshwater Lake, a good place to see wildlife in early evening. Just outside town, **Cape Smokey Lodge** *(902-285-2778. July-Aug.; adm. fee)* runs a chairlift (20 minutes each way) up a thousand-foot vertical slope, promising breathtaking views on a clear day. On top of old Smokey Mountain, a provincial park provides picnic tables, where you can feast on the views.

Continue south along the coast for about 50 miles (80 km) to **South Gut St. Anns,** settled by Highland Scots. The skirl of bagpipes can still be heard around here, thanks to the **Gaelic College of Celtic Arts and Crafts**★★ *(Cabot Trail. 902-295-3411. Craft shop and museum open July-Sept., ceilidhs held July-Aug. Wed. p.m.; adm. fee for ceilidhs),* North America's only Gaelic college. The Great Hall of the Clans contains exhibits on Scottish history and culture; also see demonstrations of traditional weaving and instrument-making, music, and dance. August events include the Highland Gathering, the Fiddlers Festival, and the multi-day Gaelic Mod. The craft shop stocks nearly 300 tartans; kilts are custom-made and shipped anywhere.

Buoys near Louisbourg

Drive east on Trans-Canada 105 into Cape Breton's urban-industrial region, center of fish processing, coal mining, and steel manufacturing. After 23 miles (37 km), drive south on Hwy. 125 to Sydney, then turn south on Hwy. 22—the Mira Road, named after the much sung river—to Louisbourg and ❹ **Fortress of Louisbourg National Historic Site★★** *(902-733-2280. June-Sept.; adm. fee).* Take a break and plan to spend at least four hours to a full day here at the fortress.

In 1713 the French established a trade and military center here, where a microcosm of 18th-century French society flourished until the British destroyed it in 1760. About a fifth of the original town, including ramparts, streets, and more than 50 buildings, has been authentically re-created to the year 1744, when Louisbourg was at its prime. Costumed interpreters assume the roles of actual residents. Also here are ruins, restaurants, a bakery and a tavern, a museum and other exhibits, plus special events.

If the weather is cooperative (it's often foggy in Louisbourg, but clear up the coast), take scenic Rte. 255 north about 37 miles (60 km) to the old coal-mining city of Glace Bay. Along this coast in the early 1900s, Italian inventor Guglielmo Marconi built three transatlantic wireless stations. Detour to **Baleine,** a beautiful spot where aviator Beryl Markham crash-landed during her 1936 transatlantic flight. Press on through Main-à-Dieu (MAN-adoo) and along Mira Bay, keeping an eye out for wading herons and various shorebirds.

At one time ❺ **Glace Bay** boasted 12 collieries. None now remain, but on a chilly night the place smells faintly, nostalgically, of coal fires. Visit **Cape Breton Miners' Museum and Miners' Village★** *(42 Birkley St. 902-849-4522. Closed Sat.-Sun. Sept.-May; adm. fee),* where exhibits tell of the industry's history and culture. Also tour an on-site historic mine, take a simulated trip through a present-day mine, and visit a village miner's house, company store, and restaurant. Across town, **Marconi National Historic Site** *(Timmerman St. June–mid-Sept.)* honors the man who proved it possible to transmit messages across the Atlantic using electromagnetic waves rather than wires. The bluff-top site of his 1902 station features a model of the original station, the cement foundations of the old one, technical exhibits, and the Wireless Hall of Fame.

Return to Canso Causeway via scenic Hwy. 4, or take the speedier Hwy. 125 and Trans-Canada 105. To go on to Newfoundland, follow signs to the ferry in North Sydney.

Giant MacAskill

Northeast of South Gut St. Anns, Rte. 312 leads off Trans-Canada 105 to **Englishtown** and the **Giant MacAskill Museum** *(902-929-2875. Adm. fee).* A small exhibit honors former resident Angus MacAskill (1825-1863), the famous, "Gentle Giant," who stood 7 feet 9 inches and weighed in at 425 pounds. On display are his bed, chair, coat, and 16-inch-long boots, as well as some yellowed articles and photographs.

Halifax Circle★★

● **340 miles/550 km** ● **4 to 5 days** ● **June to October**

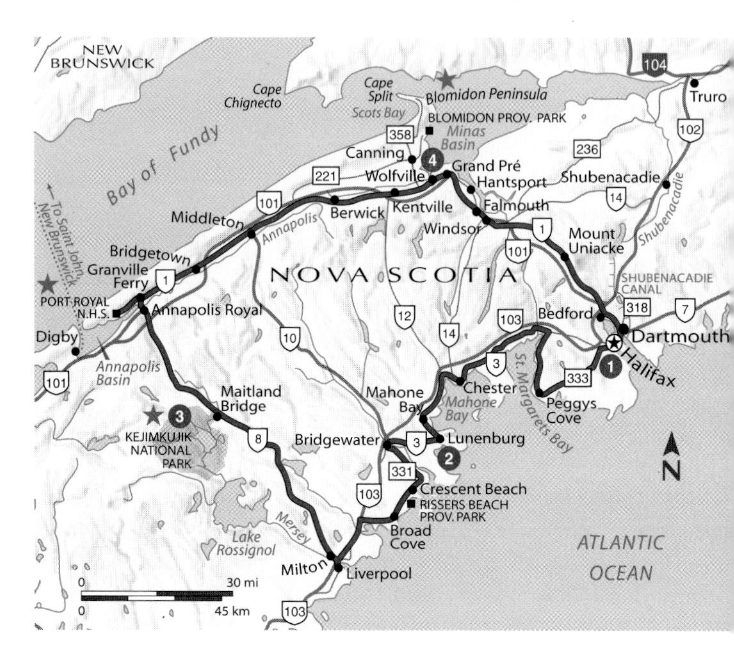

This tour offers a sampling of some of the best of mainland Nova Scotia, beginning with an urban start in the lively, old port of Halifax and moving along the scenic south shore beside the Atlantic coast, with its moored fishing boats in rocky coves; island-studded coastline; and long, narrow inlets and broad, blue bays against spruce hills. Next the drive crosses the forested interior to the Bay of Fundy at Annapolis Royal, Nova Scotia's oldest European settlement. The legacy of early French farmers is preserved on the north shore in the Acadian language, customs, and acres of dike lands. Looping back to Halifax, this route travels east through the villages and towns of the beautiful Annapolis Valley to the Minas Basin, where the world's highest tides expose vast mudflats and create a tidal bore.

Public Gardens, Halifax

❶ **Halifax★** *(Visitor Center 902-490-5946)* underwent a renaissance this past decade, making it one of the most vibrant cities in the Atlantic provinces. Along with restaurants, galleries, museums, theater, film, and music, it hosts a circus of summer festivals, including the Nova Scotia

International Tattoo *(1st week in July),* the duMaurier Ltd. Atlantic Jazz Festival *(mid- to late July),* and the International Buskers Festival *(mid-Aug.).*

The city's roots go back to 1749, when Governor Edward Cornwallis fortified a settlement here to defend the prized harbor—one of the world's finest natural harbors—against the French based at Cape Breton's Fortress of Louisbourg (see p. 33). Nineteenth-century British fortifications still command the hill. You can spend hours exploring inside and outside the walls of the star-shaped **Halifax Citadel National Historic Site★** *(Mid-May–mid-Oct., grounds open year- round; adm. fee).* Completed in 1856, this astonishing stone complex features an army museum, an audio-visual history presentation, military drills, and more.

Halifax waterfront

Nearby, stroll through the 17-acre **Public Gardens★** *(Spring Garden Rd. at S. Park St.),* which took root as a private garden in the 1750s and now contains some of the loveliest Victorian gardens around, with free concerts in the gazebo on summer Sunday afternoons. Walk a block north to the **Nova Scotia Museum of Natural History★** *(1747 Summer St. 902-424-7353. Closed Mon. mid-Oct.–May; adm. fee in summer),* a big, fun, very interactive discovery center, with changing exhibits on archaeology and ethnicity. An array of cafés, restaurants, shops, and galleries line Spring Garden Road and Barrington Street, downtown's main arteries. You'll find the bohemian student district around Argyle and Blowers Streets.

Halifax's main sights are clustered conveniently on or near the refurbished waterfront, including a section called Historic Properties. Just off the harborside boardwalk promenade, the **Maritime Museum of the Atlantic**★ *(1675 Lower Water St. 902-424-7490. Closed Mon. mid-Oct.–May; adm. fee in summer)* contains exhibits on the navy, sailing ships and steamships, the *Titanic* and the Halifax Explosion (take the time to view the excellent video), small craft and ship models, a restored ship's chandlery, plus historic vessels. Be sure to visit the nearby **Art Gallery of Nova Scotia**★★ *(1741 Hollis St. at Cheapside. 902-424-7542. Closed Mon.; adm. fee),* which harbors historical and contemporary exhibits by provincial, North American, and European artists, including an acclaimed collection of folk art. On the historic Grand Parade stands **St. Paul's Church.** Built in 1750, it's Canada's oldest Anglican church and Halifax's oldest building.

If it's Saturday morning, don't miss the fabulous **Brewery Market**★ *(Lower Water and Hollis Sts.)* in the labyrinthine, old brick brewery. Along with fruits and vegetables, this lively farmers' market offers everything from dried flowers to smoked fish.

More sights await across the harbor in Halifax's sister city of **Dartmouth** *(Convention & Visitors Bureau 902-466-2875).* Visit the **Quaker Whaler House** *(59 Ochterloney St. 902-464-2253. June–Labor Day; donation),* one of the oldest houses in town, built around 1785 by Nantucket Quakers. At Lock No. 3 of the historic Shubenacadie Canal—the 70-mile-long inland waterway linking Halifax Harbour and the Bay of Fundy—**Fairbanks Centre** *(54 Locks Rd., Port Wallace. 902-462-1826. Mid-May–Labor Day, grounds open year-round)* features restored locks, a working scale model, archaeological artifacts, and canalside trails. To learn about the history and culture of Nova Scotia's black community, visit the museum and library at the **Black Cultural Centre for Nova Scotia** *(1149 Main St., Westphal. 902-434-6223. Mon.-Fri.).*

Leave Halifax via Hwy. 3, quickly reaching the turnoff for Rte. 333 to **Peggys Cove,** a picturesque Nova Scotia fishing village (the one you see on all the posters). The real scenics begin at the blue Head of St. Margarets Bay. Wind along for 20-odd miles (32 km), then detour into the charming village of **Chester,** a well-heeled, New England-like, boating resort since the mid-1800s, offering restaurants, galleries, shops, and charming Victorians. Drive for about 14 miles (23 km) through a string of little communities, none so spiffy as the arty resort of

The Halifax Explosion

In 1917 Halifax was a wartime boomtown. The port bustled with Europe-bound convoys of supply ships and warship escorts, and the city was crowded with troops, sailors, workers, and their families. On December 6, the French ship *Mont Blanc,* loaded with tons of explosives, collided in the harbor with the Norwegian cargo vessel *Imo* and immediately burst into flames. Just before 9:05 a.m., the ship exploded. The largest man-made blast before the atom bomb shattered windows over 50 miles away and sent shock waves as far as Cape Breton. It killed more than 1,700 people, wounded thousands more, and damaged or destroyed 13,630 homes, leaving 6,000 homeless. Ultimately, both ships were judged at fault, so no one was blamed. Every December 6 at 9:05 a.m., the memorial bells at Fort Needham ring out across Halifax and Dartmouth in memory.

Fisheries Museum of the Atlantic, Lunenburg

Mahone Bay, which suddenly appears across the cove like a 19th-century mirage. A showcase of exemplary architecture of that period, the place is a veritable hive of studios, galleries, upscale shops, and tantalizing eateries.

Keep going south along Hwy. 3 toward ❷ **Lunenburg★** *(Visitor Center, Blockhouse Hill. 902-634-3656).* Established in 1753 by the British and settled by German, Swiss, and French farmers who then turned to the sea, Lunenburg has a long and lusty seafaring history. Home of the famous schooner *Bluenose,* Lunenburg is still a working town—with an artistic flair. Explore the old town, a national historic district of narrow streets and vintage architecture *(self-guided walking tour map available at Visitor Center).* Don't miss the **Fisheries Museum of the Atlantic★** *(68 Bluenose Dr. 902-634-4794. Closed Sat.-Sun. mid-Oct.–May; adm. fee).* Housed in a former fish-processing plant, the complex features an aquarium and exhibits on everything from rum-running to dory building, whaling to winds, plus an authentic banks schooner and side trawler.

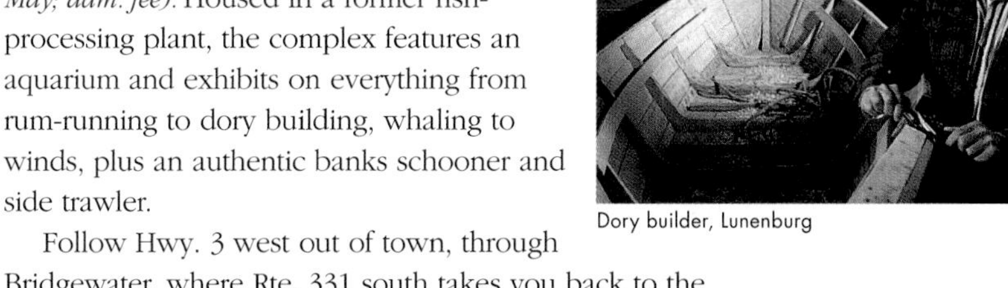
Dory builder, Lunenburg

Follow Hwy. 3 west out of town, through Bridgewater, where Rte. 331 south takes you back to the coast along a beautiful stretch of the **Lighthouse Trail.** Magic happens here on a summer's evening, when everything is drenched in pure golden light, creating some excruciatingly perfect moments. Stop and stretch your legs at **Rissers Beach Provincial Park** along the lovely boardwalk **Salt Marsh Trail.** You'll be happy you did.

After nearly 28 miles (45 km), turn south on Hwy. 103 to **Liverpool★** *(Visitor Center, Henry Hensey Dr. 902-354-5421).* From 1776 through the War of 1812, Liverpool prospered as the home port of the Privateers—the infamous, seafaring militia of swashbuckling buccaneers. The self-guided walking tour *(map available at Visitor Center)* leads to the **1766 Perkins House** *(105 Main St. 902-354-4058. June–mid-Oct.)* and the adjacent **Queens County Museum** *(109 Main St. 902-354-4058. Closed Sun. mid-Oct.–May),* featuring exhibits on regional history. On an artful note, visit the **Savage Studio & Gallery** *(611 Mersey Point. 902-354-5431. Call for hours)* of artist Roger Savage.

Canoeing at Kejimkujik National Park

Continue along, taking Hwy. 8 north out of town, across the glassy Mersey River and through Milton. Designated the Kejimkujik Scenic Drive, the route roughly follows part of a 200-year-old wilderness trail between the Atlantic and the Bay of Fundy. For the next 42 miles (67 km), you're in the woods, rolling over a sea of small and fertile glacial hills, called drumlins. Beautiful ❸ **Kejimkujik National Park★** *(Maitland Bridge. 902-682-2772. Adm. fee in summer),* "Kedge" for short, is primarily a 147-square-mile back-country preserve of forests and waterways long used by the native Mi'kmaq. Drive-by visitors can still enjoy a riverside stroll, a short hike, a lakeside picnic, or a swim. The Visitor Center, worth a stop, offers exhibits on the region's rich natural and cultural history.

Another 30 miles (47 km) north and you emerge from the woods into historic **Annapolis Royal** *(Visitor Center in Tidal Exhibit Centre, Hwy. 1E. 902-532-5454),* Nova Scotia's colonial capital on the Acadian coast. In 1605 French explorers Samuel de Champlain and Sieur de Monts established here what they called Port Royal, Nova Scotia's oldest European settlement. The British later renamed it Annapolis to honor Queen Anne.

A treasure trove of historic architecture, small museums, galleries, shops, and eateries, the town of Annapolis Royal is made for walking *(self-guided tour info. available at Visitor Center).* For an entertaining social history of the town, join the **Garrison Graveyard Candlelight Tour★** *(Tours leave from Fort Anne Museum. 902-532-2397. Mid-June–mid-Oct. Thurs. and Sun.; fee for tours).* Your guide can tell you some stories about the dearly, and not so dearly, departed buried here as far back as 1720. **Fort Anne National Historic Site★** *(295 St. George St. 902-532-2397. Site open year-round, museum open mid-June–mid-Oct.; adm. fee)* preserves 1702 earthworks, the powder magazine, and the British officers' quarters—now a museum—of this strategic French garrison, capital of Acadia from about 1635 to 1710, when it fell to the British.

Nearby, the magnificent **Annapolis Royal Historic Gardens★** *(441 St. George St. 902-532-7018. Mid-May–Oct.; adm. fee)* features 10 acres of theme gardens and historic horticultural displays overlooking a wetlands wildfowl sanctuary. See what's on at the **King's Theatre Summer Festival** *(209 St. George St. 902-532-5466. July-Aug.; adm. fee)* and the lively **Farmers & Traders Market** *(Opposite public wharf. July-Aug. Wed. p.m., mid-May–mid-Oct. Sat. a.m.).*

Follow Hwy. 1 northeast across the Annapolis River, stopping en route to tour the **Tidal Generating Station,** the only one in North America, which churns out one percent of Nova Scotia's power. Hook a sharp left at the sign for Port Royal and follow Main Street through **Granville Ferry.** The **North Hills Museum** *(902-532-2168. June–mid-Oct.; donation)* exhibits a banker's stunning collection of Georgian furniture, silver, ceramics, and paintings in his finely restored, 1760s farmhouse.

Just 5 miles (8 km) past here, **Port Royal National Historic Site★** *(902-532-2898. Mid-May–mid-Oct.; adm. fee)* marks the site of the original French settlement, l'Habitation, breathtakingly set above the river with a clear straightaway

Hurley to Hockey

Although as Canadian as the maple leaf, the origin of ice hockey in the country is not clearly documented. Windsor, Nova Scotia, is the acknowledged birthplace of the sport, probably some time around 1830. King's College School students adapted hurley, an Irish stick-and-ball game, to the ice on Long Pond. Over the next 50 years, ice hurley evolved into the game of hockey in Nova Scotia, as well as in Montreal and Kingston, Ontario, using Mi'kmaq-made wooden sticks and pucks. Organized teams played in the 1882 Montreal Winter Carnival Tournament, and by 1893 hockey was being played seriously from coast to coast.

toward the Annapolis Basin. An amiable costumed guide greets you at the entrance to the reproduced wooden trading post, containing reconstructed living quarters, the forge, the bakery, and the common room.

Return east on Hwy. 1. The road bisects the long, broad Annapolis Valley, the heart of Nova Scotia's apple country. After driving about 68 miles (109 km), you reach ❹ **Wolfville** *(Visitor Center, 11 Willow Ave. 902-542-7000),* a colorful little college town and the region's cultural center. The small **Acadia University Art Gallery** *(Beveridge Arts Centre, Main St. and Highland Ave. 902-542-2200 ext. 1373)* exhibits work by mostly Nova Scotia artists. Stroll around and ogle the town's vintage houses along the self-guided Heritage Walking Tour. From June to September, the Atlantic Theatre Festival *(902-542-4242)* showcases plays that range from Greek to contemporary.

If time permits, consider a 20-mile (32-km) side trip up the high, rugged promontory of **Blomidon Peninsula★** *(Hwy. 1 W to Rte. 358 N)*—the home, according to Mi'kmaq legend, of the great man-god Glooscap. You wind through Canning, then up the ancient North Mountain Ridge where the dramatic sweep of Scots Bay takes you by surprise. Reminiscent of Ireland's west coast, long paddocks and green pastures here run to the rocky beach. Low tide exposes the stones and mud-flats. It is a transcendent thing to watch the sun melt into the sea here. Bring a bottle of wine, find a drift-wood perch, and wait for the show.

Orchard stroll, Annapolis Valley

Follow the Cape Split road to the end and take the popular hike out to **Cape Split** *(8 miles round-trip, about four hours walking time),* where the tide comes in with an audible roar. Also worth a visit is **Blomidon Provincial Park** *(From Canning follow Rte. 221 and signs. 902-582-7319. Mid-June–mid-Oct.)* overlooking the Minas Basin and famed for the world's highest tides.

Resume your eastward course on Hwy. 1. Just beyond Wolfville, stop and visit the **Grand-Pré National Historic Site** *(Grand-Pre Rd. 902-542-3631. Site open year-round, Memorial Church open mid-May–mid-Oct.).* This Acadian mecca marks the site of the 1755 expulsion of the

Dusk over Cape Blomidon

Acadians by the British, and symbolizes the rebirth and survival of their culture, with a beautiful memorial church and commemorative gardens.

Drive east on Hwy. 1 for about a mile (1.6 km) to Hwy. 101 and **Windsor** *(Visitor Information Centre, 31 Colonial Rd. 902-798-2690),* which has the distinction of sitting exactly halfway between the North Pole and the Equator. It also claims fame as the birthplace of ice hockey (see sidebar p. 39), with exhibits at the **Windsor Hockey Heritage Centre** *(Water St. 902-798-1800. Donation).* **Fort Edward National Historic Site** *(Fort Edward St. 902-542-3631. Site open year-round, blockhouse open mid-June–Aug.)* preserves Canada's oldest blockhouse, built by the British in 1750. Among the town's most impressive estates, now provincial museums, are the 1836 **Haliburton House Museum★** *(414 Clifton Ave. 902-798-2915. June–mid-Oct.),* home of humorist Judge Thomas Chandler Haliburton, creator of the inimitable Sam Slick; and the 1891 **Shand House Museum** *(389 Avon St. 902-798-8213. June–mid-Oct.),* a repository of Victoriana. East of town, travel along Hwy. 14 to Rte. 236, and the **Tidal View Farm,** a fine place to see the tidal bore—the first wave of the incoming tide *(check tide schedule at the Visitor Center).*

Circle back toward Halifax on Hwy. 1, stopping at the **Uniacke Estate Museum Park** *(Mount Uniacke, Old Windsor Hwy. 902-866-0032. June–mid-Oct.),* about 30 miles (48 km) south. Enjoy a walk through this outstanding 1815 Georgian-style country estate, packed with antiques, or wander its pleasant nature trails.

The Island

● 310 miles/500 km ● 4 to 5 days ● Mid-June to mid-October ● Ferry from Caribou, Nova Scotia, to Wood Islands, P.E.I. (902-566-3838. Fare), or Cape Tormentine, N.B., to Borden-Carleton, P.E.I. (902-437-2030. Fare). In June 1997 a new bridge will cross from Cape Jourimaine, N.B., to Borden-Carleton, P.E.I.

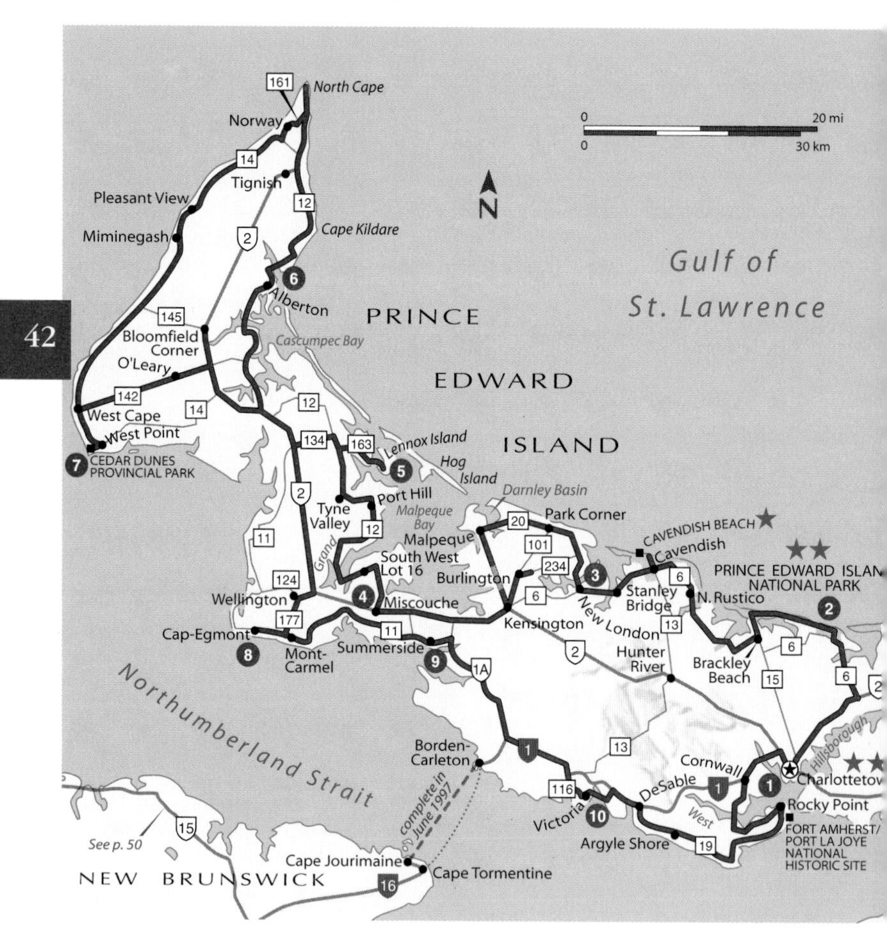

For all its hyped image as the Land of Anne (Anne of Green Gables, that is, as created by favorite island author Lucy Maud Montgomery), the diversity of green and fragrant Prince Edward Island, called P.E.I., or simply the Island, stems from its patchwork of Mi'kmaq, Acadian, and Scotch-Irish heritage. From the friendly, tree-shaded capital of Charlottetown, wend along the north shore's dunes and the red cliffs of beautiful Prince Edward Island National Park, past craft shops, picturesque fishing villages, endless potato fields, and clay roads rolling to blue waters. Sample a lobster supper, then trace the western peninsula from tip to windy tip, circling back along the Northumberland Strait to town.

Canada's smallest provincial capital, named in 1765 after King George III's wife, ❶ **Charlottetown★★** *(Visitor Center, 178 Water St. 902-368-4444)* can claim the large honor of being Canada's birthplace. In 1864 delegates met in what is now **Province House National Historic Site★** *(Richmond and Great George Sts. 902-566-7626. Closed Sat.-Sun. Nov.-May; donation)* to discuss a union that, in 1867, became the Dominion of Canada. The current home of the Legislative Assembly contains exhibits and interpretive programs. Next door, the massive, modern **Confederation Centre of the Arts★★** *(145 Richmond St. 902-566-1267)* holds three theaters and the **Art Gallery and Museum** *(Closed Mon.; adm. fee)* of contemporary and historic Canadian art, including a collection of portraits by celebrated Island artist Robert Harris. Nearby, have a peek at the imposing **St. Dunstan's Basilica** *(Great George St.)*, with its exquisite rose and unusual windows and carved ceiling figureheads.

Brackley Beach, Prince Edward Island National Park

Charlottetown's compactness is part of its appeal, and its sights and lovely side streets are best enjoyed on foot *(walking tour map available at Visitor Center)*. The city's only public historic house is situated adjacent to **Victoria Park.** Designed by William Critchlow Harris, the 1877 **Beaconsfield★** *(2 Kent St. 902-368-6600. Closed Sat. and Mon. Sept.–mid-June; adm. fee)* preserves the exquisite 25-room Victorian mansion of wealthy shipbuilder James Peake, Jr. Harris created another gem in his nearby 1888 **All Soul's**

Chapel★ *(Rochford Sq.),* adjoining St. Peter's Cathedral. This national historic site contains 18 magnificent murals by the architect's brother, Robert Harris.

Once Charlottetown's shipbuilding and shipping center, **Peake's Wharf★** now draws crowds with shops, cafés, street theater, and schooner tours. **Confederation Landing Park** interprets historical events on the site where the Fathers of Confederation landed in 1864. For some local flavor, visit the **Farmers' Market** *(Belvedere and University Aves. July-Aug. Wed. and Sat.-Sun.).* Or view professional harness racing at **Charlottetown Driving Park** *(Kensington Rd. 902-892-6823. June-Aug. Mon., Thurs., and Sat.; Sept.-May Thurs., Sat.; adm. fee),* site of Old Home Week *(2nd week in Aug.),* featuring eastern Canada's best drivers and fastest horses. Other major events in town include the P.E.I. Jazz & Blues Society Festival *(late July),* Festival of the Fathers *(late Aug.),* and Festival of the Arts *(mid-Sept.).*

Head north on Hwy. 2 to Rte. 6 and **2 Prince Edward Island National Park★★** *(902-672-6350. Adm. fee),* a skinny, 25-mile-long preserve along the north coast distinguished by a line of grassy dunes up to 59 feet high, covered by marram grass. Beyond stretch some of the warmest ocean waters north of the Carolinas, thanks to the Gulf Stream. Drive along the coastal Gulf Shore Parkway to the park's eastern landmark, **Dalvay By The Sea** *(902-672-2048).* Completed in 1896 by Alexander MacDonald, who made his fortune in American oil, the elegant Victorian mansion has aged well into a grand old inn.

Leaving the park near Brackley Beach, keep driving west on Rte. 6 to **Cavendish** *(Visitor Center 902-963-2391),* where Green Gables nostalgia is a booming industry. Visit the **Site of Lucy Maud Montgomery's Cavendish Home★** *(Rte. 6. 902-963-2231. June–mid-Oct.; adm. fee),* where the author lived with her grandparents and wrote her first four novels. Stroll the grounds, see the little museum, and find her garden grave in nearby **Cavendish Cemetery.** Then walk the Haunted Wood Trail, or drive to **Green Gables House★** *(Rte. 6. 902-672-6350. May-Oct.; adm. fee.),* Montgomery's cousins' farmhouse, furnished as described in her books.

Backtrack briefly and take Hwy. 13 north to the park's distinctive western section at **Cavendish Beach★.** The road dead-ends at a breathtaking overlook on hummocky dunes, swirling red sandstone bluffs, and the gorgeous

Linked at Last

No longer will passengers wait in line for the ritual 45-minute ferry crossing from New Brunswick. In June 1997, after more than a century of schemes and years of hot debate, the Island gains a fixed link—and a 12-minute drive—to the mainland. Confederation Bridge (known as the Link), a unique, albeit controversial, 7.9-mile (12.9-km) concrete span, connects Cape Jourimaine, New Brunswick, and Borden-Carleton, P.E.I. The cost: over $800 million—and, to many people, tradition.

sweep of beach below *(access just west, off Gulf Shore Pkwy.).*

Continue west on Rte. 6, past endless fields of golden barley, neat rows of potatoes, and great cylinders of baled hay. Views are at a premium here, where the higher land affords long vistas across the New London Bay and the Gulf of St. Lawrence. At **Stanley Bridge,** the quirky, old-fashioned **PEI Marine Aquarium** *(Rte. 6. 902-892-2203. Mid-June–mid-Sept.; adm. fee)* contains tanks of regional marine species, 750 mounted birds, a large collection of mounted butterflies, and a pool of entertaining harbor seals.

In nearby ❸ **New London,** the **Lucy Maud Montgomery Birthplace** *(Rtes. 6 and 20. 902-886-2099. Late May–mid-Oct.; adm. fee)* preserves the cottage where Montgomery was born on November 30, 1874. Displays include period furnishings, the author's wedding dress, scrapbooks, and other personal effects.

Pick up Rte. 20 and continue past corduroy fields punctuated by steeply gabled farmhouses and bread and potato stands, to **Park Corner,** a great, glorious sweep of undulating green encircled by the horizon. Watch on

Farmlands near North Rustico

the right for the **Lucy Maud Montgomery Heritage Museum★** *(Rte. 20. 902-886-2807. June-Sept.; adm. fee).* The 1879 Victorian farmhouse of Montgomery's grandfather, Senator "Big Donald" Montgomery, is cluttered with original furniture, family heirlooms, and artifacts immortalized in Lucy

Old fisherman harbor, Malpeque

Maud's novels, plus a political gallery. Across the road, visit the **Anne of Green Gables Museum at Silver Bush** *(Rte. 20. 902-436-7329 or 800-665-2663. June-Oct., by appt. rest of year; adm. fee).* Montgomery called her aunt and uncle's 1872 farmhouse "the wonder castle of my childhood." She was married here in 1911. The museum features original furnishings, personal items, autographed first editions, a farm museum, an antique and craft gallery, a tearoom, and wagon rides.

For the next few miles Rte. 20 proves a stunning stretch of road. From **Malpeque,** home of world-famous oysters, continue to Kensington. Detour briefly north on Rte. 101 to Burlington, then follow Rte. 234 to **Woodleigh Replicas & Gardens**★ *(902-836-3401. June–mid-Oct.; adm. fee).* A 50-plus-year labor of love created by Anglophile Lt. Col. Ernest Johnstone, it includes some 25 large-scale (we're not talking miniatures here) and detailed (down to the last stone, beam, and buttress) re-creations of famous British landmarks and English gardens.

Return to Kensington and drive west on Hwy. 2 to the Island's Acadian region. At ❹ **Miscouche** (MIS-cush), the small but colorful **Acadian Museum of P.E.I**★ *(Hwy. 2. 902-432-2880. Daily late June–Labor Day, Mon.-Fri. rest of year; adm. fee)* presents the Island's rich Acadian heritage. During the annual Festival Folk-Acadie *(mid-July–mid-Aug.),* you'll also find music, crafts, lectures, and food.

Bear northwest on Rte. 12 through South West Lot 16. (When the British took P.E.I. from the French in 1758, they divided it by lottery into 67 townships, or lots, to reward

individuals for their services to the Crown.) At **Port Hill,** see the **Green Park Shipbuilding Museum and Historic Yeo House**★ *(Rte. 12. 902-831-2206. Mid-June–Labor Day; adm. fee).* During the 1800s, the Yeos, the island's most powerful shipbuilding family, ran a booming business here. The small museum tells the story of this major industry and its leading players. Footpaths lead to a re-created shipyard and to the restored 1865 estate of James Yeo, Jr.

Continue west along Rte. 12 to Rte. 163 and the causeway that, since 1973, has linked the mainland and the Mi'kmaq reserve, established in 1912 on ❺ **Lennox Island. MicMac First Nation Crafts** *(2 Sweetgrass Trail. 902-831-2653. June-Sept.)* sells trademark ash baskets and other items. Be sure to see the murals and artifacts in the administrative building and at historic 1895 **Saint Anne's Parish Church.** Elsewhere you can see the old peat bogs, now rendered useless by saltwater infiltration.

Twist northwest along Rtes. 12 and 134 and Hwy. 2, then rejoin Rte. 12. This is a beautiful, watery land, probed by the fingers of Cascumpec Bay. In ❻ **Alberton,** the 1877 courthouse contains the **Alberton Museum** *(Rte. 12. 902-853-4048. Late June–Sept.; adm. fee)* and exhibits on P.E.I.'s famous silver fox industry, begun here in 1894.

The sense of remoteness increases as you travel up the western peninsula. Land's end is at blustery **North Cape,** reputedly the Island's windiest spot and a logical location for the **Atlantic Wind Test Site**★ for new wind-diesel technologies. A stand of experimental windmills towers and hums above the treeless plateau, dwarfing the 1866 lighthouse. The site's **Interpretive Centre** *(902-882-2991. Late May–early Oct., tours of test site July-Aug.; adm. fee)* contains exhibits on alternative energy and the region's history, natural history, industry, and culture, plus an aquarium. Offshore, gulf and strait currents collide on one of the world's longest, most treacherous, natural rock reefs, where seals and seabirds congregate.

Potato field along Rte. 142

Mossing

There's nothing like a good, old-fashioned nor'wester to send the townsfolk of Miminegash, whole families, in fact, scrambling—on horseback, in trucks or boats, on foot with gloms (scoops)—to harvest the loosened Irish moss. The seaweed, which grows in the intertidal zone between the deep kelp and the rockweed, contains a valuable natural gel called carrageenan—a tasteless, noncaloric, starchlike substance used mostly to thicken dairy products, but also as an emulsifier in toothpaste, paint, shampoo, wine, cough syrup, and many other products. P.E.I. produces almost a quarter of the world's supply.

Backtrack to Rte. 161 toward Norway, then drive south on Rte. 14, tracing the more rugged western shore, where the cliffs reveal the rocky plateau underlying the cape. Life is harsher here on the edge, where weathered farmhouses stand like sentries to the wind on treeless bluff tops and cows graze beside stacked lobster traps. Everywhere the sea is omnipresent.

French names reappear on mailboxes as you drive south across the empty plain into **Miminegash.** It even sounds like the kind of place where people harvest Irish moss for a living (see sidebar this page). Learn all about it—the plant, the tradition, the industry—at the **Irish Moss Interpretive Centre★** *(Rte. 14. 902-882-4313. Late June–Sept.; adm. fee)* and sample seaweed pie at the adjacent café. Down by the harbor you might see the lacy, florid moss spread to dry, and trucks unloading and baling the stuff.

Continue down the coast past tiny fishing communities and tenacious potato fields to **West Point.** At ❼ **Cedar Dunes Provincial Park** *(Off Rte. 14),* visit the restored 1875 **West Point Lighthouse** *(902-859-3605 or 800-764-6854. June-Sept.; fee for tours),* now a unique restaurant and inn containing a museum of lighthouse history. Behind the light, wander through the coastal woods along "fairy walks" (but beware of ravenous mosquitoes).

Backtrack to Rte. 142 and drive inland to **O'Leary,** home of the **Prince Edward Island Potato Museum★** *(22 Parkview Dr. 902-859-2039. June–mid-Oct.; adm. fee),* which celebrates the humble potato, the island's economic mainstay, with extensive exhibits. Watch for the annual July Prince Edward Island Potato Blossom Festival.

A few miles beyond take Hwy. 2 north to **Bloomfield Corner,** home of the famous **MacAusland's Woollen Mills Ltd.** *(902-859-3005. Mon.-Fri.),* now into its fourth generation. Visit the old working mill and observe the whole process.

Return southeast on Hwy. 2, turning onto Rte. 124 toward Wellington, and then Rte. 177 toward **Mont Carmel.** You're back in French country now. West along Rte. 11, **Acadian Pioneer Village** *(902-854-2227. June–mid-Sept.; adm. fee)* contains a small, reproduction historical village. Down the road in 8 **Cap-Egmont,** see the unique **Bottle Houses** *(902-854-2987. Mid-June–mid-Sept.; adm. fee),* created from more than 25,000 light-catching bottles. The setting is lovely, with flower gardens and sea views.

Head east on Rte. 11 to 9 **Summerside** *(Visitor Center 902-436-6692).* The **Eptek National Exhibition Centre**★ *(130 Harbour Dr. 902-888-8373. Closed Mon. Sept.-June; adm. fee)* exhibits mostly Canadian crafts, fine art, and history. The **International Fox Museum and Hall of Fame** *(286 Fitzroy St. 902-436-2400. May-Sept. Mon.-Sat.; donation)* presents the history of P.E.I.'s renowned silver fox industry. Catch the harness races at historic **Summerside Raceway** *(477 Notre Dame St. 902-436-7221. Wed. eve. June–mid-Oct.; adm. fee),* up and running since 1886.

Capturing Victoria harbor

Continue down the coast to Hwy. 116 and 10 **Victoria,** a charming 19th-century seaside village. See what's on at **Victoria Playhouse** *(902-658-2025. Adm. fee)* and then shore up on community history at the **Victoria Seaport Museum** *(In the lighthouse on Blue Heron Dr. 902-658-2602. July-Aug.).*

Rejoin Trans-Canada 1 east to Rte. 19, which leads along the lovely Argyle Shore, named by homesick Scottish settlers. Soon you'll arrive at **Fort Amherst/Port la Joye National Historic Site** *(Off Rte. 19, Rocky Point. 902-672-6350. June–mid-Oct.; adm. fee).* In 1720 the French founded P.E.I.'s first permanent European settlement, called Port la Joye. In 1758 the British captured the area and built this fort; only the earthworks remain. Rte. 19 and Trans-Canada 1 lead back to Charlottetown.

Fundy to Kouchibouguac

● 185 miles/300 km ● 3 to 4 days ● Mid-June through October

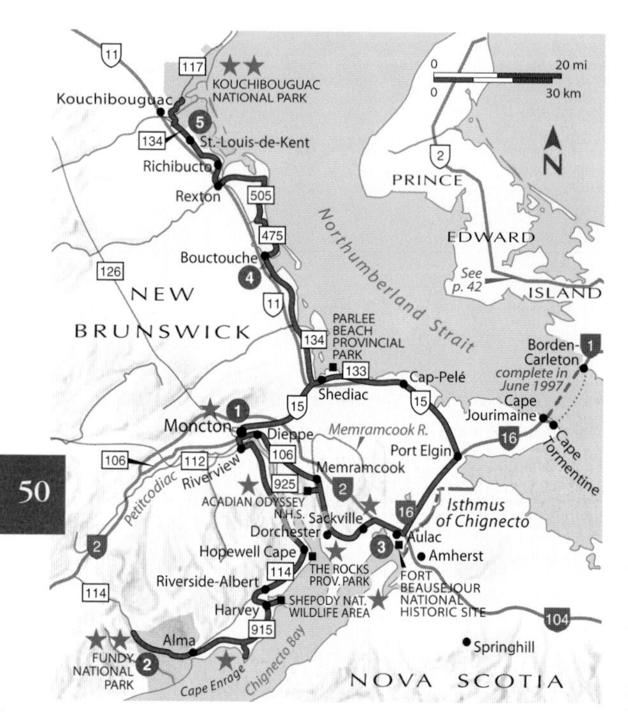

The southeastern corner of New Brunswick is rich in natural and ethnic history. From busy, bicultural Moncton, this drive takes a side trip down the rugged Fundy coast, shaped by the world's highest tides, visiting a fine shorebird reserve and splendid Fundy National Park. Amid the lush fields of the Memramcook region, discover a preserve of Acadian history. Then loop up the lovely Acadian coast.

Traditionally the rail and transportation hub of the Maritimes, ❶ **Moncton**★ *(Visitor Center, 655 Main St. 506-853-3590 or 800-363-4558. Walking tour info. available)* has a decided French flair, thanks to the University of Moncton, Canada's largest French language university outside Quebec. On a nice day, Main Street buzzes with activity. Permanent exhibits at the **Moncton Museum** *(20 Mountain Rd. 506-856-4383. Donation)* trace the city's history and development, from Mi'kmaq and pioneer settlements through the shipbuilding and rail eras. The university's **Acadian Museum**★ *(Clement Cormier Bldg. 506-858-4088. Closed Mon. Oct.-May; donation)* beautifully portrays the history and culture of the Acadians from the 1600s to the present through artifacts, photographs, and art. An adjoining art gallery showcases contemporary Canadian art.

Drop by the **Moncton Market** *(120 Westmorland St. off Main St. Aug.-mid-Sept. Sat. and Wed.)* for fresh produce, food, and crafts. The Moncton Jazz & Blues Festival *(506-853-3540 or 800-363-4558)* heats up the downtown annually in late June and early July.

Allow a full day for an obligatory side trip down the Fundy coast. Follow Rte. 114 (disparaged by locals as the Fundy Cowpath) south to **The Rocks Provincial Park★** *(Rte. 114, Hopewell Cape. 506-734-3429. Mid-May–mid-Oct.; adm. fee)* to see the amazing "flowerpot" rocks—huge sea stacks carved by the elements from the sandstone cliffs. At low tide (we're talking 42-foot tides here) you can descend to the ocean floor and explore the exposed sea caves and tunnels.

Drive another 10 miles (16 km) along the bay and pick up scenic Rte. 915 south. After a few miles, turn down Mary's Point Road to the interpretive center at the Mary's Point section of the **Shepody National Wildlife Area★** *(May-Oct.)*. This is part of the Western Hemisphere Shorebird Reserve Network, stretching from Arctic breeding grounds to South American wintering grounds. Each year between July and October, up to two million migrating shorebirds stop here to feast on Fundy's fertile mudflats before flying south, nonstop, across the ocean. The balletic swooping and circling of these tiny creatures is truly a mesmerizing sight.

Magic Mountain water park, Moncton

About 7.5 miles (12 km) farther, detour to windy and wild **Cape Enrage★** *(Cape Enrage Adventures 506-887-2273)*, where the 1850 **Cape Enrage Lightstation** commands the point, offering an exhilarating panorama of the bay and the nearly 150-foot-high cliffs. (You actually look *down* on seabirds soaring on currents.) If the tide is out, brave the steep stairs to the beach. The keeper's cottage, **Cape House,** holds a café *(506-887-2273. Late May-early Sept.)* known for its superlative haddock chowder.

Follow Rte. 915 along the beach to **Alma**. Here low tide leaves anchored boats high and dry in the mud until the returning tide releases them; you can walk for miles on the rocks and mudflats of the exposed sea-floor—heaven for rock hounds. Be sure to check the tide schedule so you don't get caught: The rising tide climbs a foot every 7 minutes, up to 39 feet in 6 hours and 13 minutes.

Dickson Falls, Fundy National Park

At the far end of town, enter ❷ **Fundy National Park★★** *(Visitor Center 506-887-6000. Adm. fee),* a small but impressively diverse preserve encompassing mostly forest, but also coast, bog, salt marsh, field, and river valley. Day-trippers can easily manage any of several delightful shorter walks or hikes, weaving through a variety of terrains on over 60 miles of trails within the park. During summer, the park offers guided beach walks and interpretive presentations in its outdoor theater.

Back in Moncton, head east on Rte. 106, passing through the commercial French-speaking town of Dieppe. But by the time you reach the municipality of **Memramcook,** you're surrounded by the fertile, historic Memramcook region, the so-called Cradle of New Acadia. This is the only part of Old Acadia, along the Fundy coast, where French settlers and their descendants have lived and farmed continuously since the turn of the 18th century. In the years following the 1755 Deportation, the valley was the center of Acadian renaissance and resettlement along New Brunswick's east coast, from Memramcook up to Caraquet. Displayed on just about anything that holds paint, the Acadian flag (French tricolors with a gold Star of Mary) symbolizes the pride and spirit of these survivors.

Bunchberry plant, the bog, Kouchibouguac National Park

Follow Rte. 925 to the **Acadian Odyssey National Historic Site** at **Monument Lefebvre★** *(Memramcook. 506-758-9783. June–mid-Oct.; adm. fee).* Adjacent to historic College Saint-Joseph—the Maritimes' first French language degree-granting institution, founded by Father Camille Lefebvre in 1864—the monument features exhibits on

Acadian history, a film about the Deportation, a magnificent theater, and a well-stocked bookstore and gift shop.

Head south on Rte. 106 through the broad, lush valley along the muddy, crooked Memramcook River, where early Acadians left their imprint in the form of dikes (*aboiteaux*), wells, and many other historic landmarks. Those marked by brown-and-yellow signs are part of the Memramcook Historical Society's **Ecomuseum** *(Ask local businesses for a self-guided driving tour map).*

At Dorchester, head east on Rte. 106 to the attractive town of **Sackville** *(Visitor Center, E. Main and King Sts. 506-364-0431. Self-guided walking tour maps available),* home of Mount Allison University. Its **Owens Art Gallery★** *(On campus off York St. 506-364-2574. Donation)* contains a large collection of historical and contemporary work by Canadian and international artists. Smack in the middle of town sprawls 55-acre **Sackville Waterfowl Park★** *(Main entrance at Main and King Sts. 506-364-0431. Tours mid-May–Aug.),* an award-winning restored wetlands preserve, with an interpretive boardwalk and trails for strolling and observing dozens of birds, mammals, and plants. During the peak shorebird migration in mid-August, the park hosts the Atlantic Waterfowl Celebration *(506-364-8080).*

On Trans-Canada 2 toward Aulac, you'll see the famous **Tantramar Marshes**—the largest reclaimed agricultural area in Canada. Early Acadian farmers started diking and draining the area in the 1670s, and by 1920 it was one of the largest hay fields in the world.

At Aulac, visit ❸ **Fort Beausejour National Historic Site** *(506-536-0720. June–mid-Oct.; adm. fee).* Anticipating the Seven Years' War, British and French forces clashed in 1755 on this barren, windblown hill, where the French had built a star-shaped fort four years earlier. Victorious, the British later used the fort during the American Revolution and the War of 1812. Along with restored casemates, interpretive displays, and exhibits, the views of the surrounding marshes and bay are superb.

Loop north via a series of scenic highways: Take Trans-Canada 16 north to Hwy. 15, then, a few miles past Cap-Pelé, head west on Rte. 133, which hugs the low-lying shore of the Northumberland Strait. Passing popular **Parlee Beach Provincial Park** and plying the beachy strip at **Shediac,** bear north on Rte. 133, which becomes Rte. 134, and drive about 20 miles (32 km) up the coast.

Highest Tides

What makes Fundy's tides the highest on earth? Simply put, it is the gravitational pull of the moon and the sun as the earth spins through space combined with the shape and size of the bay. Picture the bay as a funnel: Ocean tides rush into its wide mouth. As the water moves up the bay, it gets "squeezed" by the narrowing sides and shallowing bottom, forcing it higher up the banks. This, coupled with a resonant effect produced by the bay and the Gulf of Maine, creates the phenomenal tides. Twice a day, 100 billion tons of tidewater flood the bay—almost the combined daily flow of all the world's rivers. The highest tides—50 feet or a four-story building—occur at the bay's easternmost corner, the Minas Basin.

Real life meets fiction in 4 **Bouctouche** *(Visitor Center, Rte. 134. 506-743-8811),* home of author Antonine Maillet, who created the beloved Acadian charwoman, La Sagouine. **Le Pays de la Sagouine**★ *(Rte. 134. 506-743-1400 or 800-561-9188. Mid-June–early Sept.; adm. fee. Reservations req. for dinner theater; ask about English performances)* brings her world to life on the colorful Île-aux-puces—Fleas' Island—where the cast performs daylong theater, complemented by Acadian music and food. It's *the* place to be on Friday night for the weekly foot-stomping music jam. Don't miss the Visitor Center exhibits and excellent slide presentation.

Performer at Le Pays de la Sagouine, Bouctouche

The **Kent Museum** *(150, chemin du Convent. 506-743-5005. July-Aug.; adm. fee),* housed in an old convent school, contains exhibits on convent and Acadian life. The chapel features a hand-painted ceiling and a stunning altar.

Take pretty Rte. 475 out of town, along the beautiful shore of Bouctouche Bay, to Rte. 505 north. Continue along the strait, in and out of French fishing villages, then rejoin Rte. 134 at Rexton. Acadian flags wave along the main street of 5 **St.-Louis-de-Kent,** where the banner's designer, Marcel François Richard, was born. At the town's north end, enter **Kouchibouguac National Park**★★ *(506-876-2443. Visitor Center May–mid-Oct., park open year-round; adm. fee).* The Mi'kmaq called the area Kouchibouguac (KOO-she-BOO-gwack), meaning "river of long tides." The park occupies 97 square miles of low-lying, maritime plain, a patchwork of tranquil salt marshes and bogs, tidal rivers, freshwater ponds, mixed acadian forest, and lagoons—habitats for more than 223 species of birds, plus deer, moose, black bears, and gray seals. Stop at the Visitor Center to see the exhibits and multi-image slide shows. Among the many accessible trails, the most popular leads to **Kellys Beach,** a barrier island reached by a boardwalk spanning forest, marsh, lagoons, and dunes. Unfortunately, it draws the crowds on a warm summer day.

To complete the drive, head south along Rte. 134 or take the quicker Hwys. 11 and 15 back to Moncton.

The Saints

● **185 miles/300 km** ● **3 to 4 days** ● **Mid-June through October**

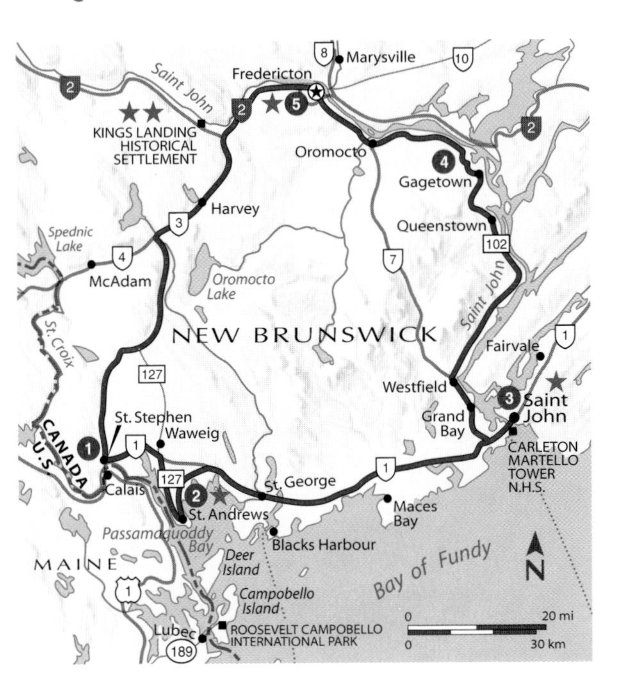

Rugged coast and verdant river valley, mixed with a good dose of arts, crafts, and history, characterize this loop tour of southwestern New Brunswick. From the border town of St. Stephen, the drive moves along the beautiful Bay of Fundy shore to the salty, old port of Saint John. It then winds along the pastoral valley of the Saint John River, through quiet villages to Fredericton, the province's friendly, cultured capital, before heading back.

Chocolate shop mascots, St. Stephen

The touristy town of ❶ **St. Stephen** *(Visitor Center 506-466-7390)* sees more comings and goings than any other border crossing in Atlantic Canada. Stop by the **Crocker Hill Studios & Gardens** *(Ledge Rd. 506-466-4251. Mid-May–*

Algonquin Resort, St. Andrews

mid-Oct., by appt. rest of year), where artists have transformed a wild hillside into a series of imaginative terraced theme gardens with ornamented walkways along the riverbanks.

Head east on Hwy. 1 to Rte. 127 south and historic ❷ **St. Andrews★** *(Welcome Centre, 46 Reed Ave. 506-529-3000. Walking tour map and guide available),* a fashionable resort during the late 1800s and early 1900s. Drop by the landmark **Algonquin Resort** *(Adolphus St. 506-529-8823 or 800-441-1414. Mid-May–mid-Oct.),* the antidote to a gray day, with crackling fires, a cozy library-cum-lounge, perfect for a dram, and kilted staff members at your service.

Nearby stands the restored **St. Andrews Blockhouse National Historic Site** *(Joe's Point Rd. 506-529-4270. June–mid-Sept.; adm. fee),* the province's last surviving blockhouse, built during the War of 1812. Also visit the 1820 **Sheriff Andrews House Provincial Historic Site** *(63 King St. 506-529-5080. Mid-June–early Sept.; donation),* where costumed guides demonstrate crafts and cooking. The 1820s continue at the **Ross Memorial Museum** *(188 Montague St. 506-529-1824. Late June–Labor Day Mon.-Sat., Labor Day–mid-Oct. Tues.-Sat.),* a house-museum displaying 19th-century furniture, decorative arts, and items collected by the Rosses on their world travels. Finally, visit the beautifully detailed 1824 **Greenock Presbyterian Church** *(Montague and Edward Sts. July-Aug.).*

Huntsman Aquarium Museum, St. Andrews

The **Huntsman Aquarium Museum★** *(Brandy Cove Rd. 506-529-1202. Mid-May–Oct.; adm. fee)* displays regional species, a very popular "touch pool" with a diversity of invertebrate marine life, and exhibits on geology, tides, aquaculture, and more. There's also an entertaining pool of harbor seals. Next visit **Minister's Island Historic Site**★ *(Guided tours only from Bar Rd. 506-529-5081. June–mid-Oct.; adm. fee),* where Canadian Pacific Railway president Sir William Van Horne built a mansion, a giant stone barn, and other amenities. It's only accessible by car at low tide. In a sylvan setting, the **Atlantic Salmon Centre** *(Off Rte. 127 north, Chamcook. 506-529-4581. Daily mid-May–Aug., Thurs.-Mon. Sept.–mid-Oct.; adm. fee)* interprets the story of the "king of fish," its biology, and conservation efforts.

Rejoin Hwy. 1 and head east. Some 60 miles (96 km) up the coast looms the smoking, big-city skyline of Saint John, Canada's oldest incorporated city, founded by United Empire Loyalists. It's also New Brunswick's manufacturing and commercial center: The signs of industry—oil, pulp, nuclear power, shipbuilding—are part of the city's slightly gritty, but appealing texture. So are the steep streets (they call downtown "uptown"); the old brick buildings; and the museums, galleries, and cafés.

On the western outskirts, view **Reversing Falls** *(Off Hwy. 1 at Bridge Rd. 506-658-2937. Roof Top Theatre 506-635-1999. Mid-May–mid-Oct.; adm. fee),* where twice a day the Saint John River subtly stops, then reverses its course as the higher and stronger bay tides ebb and flow. There's not much to see between high and low tides, so be sure to check the tide schedule. Nearby, **Carleton Martello Tower National Historic Site** *(Follow signs from Hwy. 1. 506-636-4011. June–mid-Oct.; adm. fee)* preserves a circular stone fort, which defended the city from the War of 1812 to World War II. Along with exhibits, the views are superb.

❸ **St. John**★ *(Visitor Center, Market Square. 506-658-2855)* is a great town to explore on foot *(brochures for self-guided tours available at Visitor Center).* Begin at the **New Brunswick Museum**★★ *(Market Square. 506-643-2300. Adm. fee),* an imaginative, interactive journey through the province's social and natural history. There's also a whole floor devoted to the arts and a Discovery Gallery for the kids. Next head to the **Aitken Bicentennial Exhibition Centre**★ *(20 Hazen Ave. 506-633-4870. Closed Mon. Labor Day–May),* an arts and science center, with a variety of exhibits, including the hands-on ScienceScape gallery. Also of interest is the small **Saint John Jewish Historical Museum** *(29 Wellington Row. 506-633-1833. Mon.-Fri. May-June and Sept., also open Sun. July-Aug.),* and an architectural

Campobello

The tiny Canadian island of Campobello, where President Franklin Delano Roosevelt summered as a boy and later built a 34-room "cottage," is a model of international diplomacy. A joint U.S./Canada memorial, the 2,800-acre **Roosevelt Campobello International Park** *(From St. Stephen, S on US 1 and E on Maine 189 to Lubec, then cross FDR Memorial Bridge. 506-752-2922. Cottage and Visitor Center mid-May–mid-Oct., grounds open year-round)* was created in 1964 by an international agreement signed by President Lyndon B. Johnson and Prime Minister Lester B. Pearson. It preserves the Roosevelts' home and personal effects, and the woods, bogs, and beaches he loved. The site also includes walking trails, park drives, and picnic areas.

landmark, **Loyalist House** *(120 Union St. 506-652-3590. Daily July-Aug., Mon.-Fri. June and Sept.; adm. fee),* the restored 1807 home of one of Saint John's early Loyalist families.

Save your appetite for the 1876 **Old City Market★** *(Charlotte to Germain Sts. Closed Sun.),* Canada's oldest continuing farmers market, now a national historic site and local institution, with everything from hand-knit socks to dried seaweed. Then wander through the old city's historic, arty **Trinity Royal★★** *(Bounded by King, Charlotte, Harding, and Prince William Sts.).*

Street scene, Saint John

Backtrack on Hwy. 1 to Hwy. 7 north, bearing northeast onto Rte. 102 to follow the blue and serene lower Saint John River. This old river road weaves in and out of picturesque little hamlets, past lush meadows and countless craft shops and studios. One thing you won't see anywhere else in the world—the unique network of free cable ferries crisscrossing the waterways, part of the official highway system.

The terrain becomes hillier as you near ❹ **Gagetown,** a timeless, tidy river village. Once the shiretown of Queens County and the most important trade center between Saint John and Fredericton, it was a strong contender for the new provincial capital in the 1780s. You'll still see more traffic on the river than on the narrow lanes. Along with elegant old houses, crafts are the main draw here, notably **Loomcrofters** *(Loomcroft Lane. 506-488-2400. May-Oct., by appt.),* weavers of fine tartans, headquartered in one of the oldest buildings (1761) in use along the river. The 1786 **Queens County Tilley House Museum** *(68 Front St. 506-488-2966. Mid-June–mid-Sept.; adm. fee)* preserves the birthplace of Samuel Leonard Tilley, the province's Father of Confederation, with exhibits on Queens County history.

Heading north and west on Rte. 102 you'll reach ❺ **Fredericton★** *(Visitor Center at City Hall, 397 Queen St. 506-452-9616. Walking tour map available).* New Brunswick's proud and pretty capital since 1785, it straddles a broad bend in the river. For a small city, it seems to have it all: a beautiful setting, safe streets, and outstanding architecture, art, and culture. A walker's paradise, Fredericton's premier path is **The Green★**, a 3-mile-long riverside walkway off which lie the main sights in the city's compact, historic heart.

Bagpipes sounding from Officers' Square—the old 1785 parade grounds within the **Military Compound Provincial Historic Site★**—signals the Changing of the Guard *(506-452-9508. Twice daily Tues.-Sat. July-Aug.).* Housed in the adjacent Old Officers' Quarters, the **York-Sunbury Historical Society Museum** *(506-455-6041. May–Labor Day, call for off-season hours; adm. fee)* contains exhibits on the region's civilian and military history.

In company with the **New Brunswick College of Craft and Design** *(15 Carleton St. 506-453-2305. Tours Sept.-May),* art galleries abound here, the biggest and best being **Beaverbrook Art Gallery★** *(703 Queen St. 506-458-8545. Closed Mon. Sept.-June; adm. fee).* Known for its collection of British paintings, it also exhibits work by European, Atlantic Canadian, and other North American artists.

The copper-steepled 1853 **Christ Church Cathedral★** *(Church and Brunswick Sts. 506-450-8500. Guided tours mid-June–Labor Day)* is modeled after a medieval English church, with exquisite stained-glass windows. Also of architectural note is the beautiful, restored interior of the 1882 **Provincial Legislative Assembly Building** *(Queen and St. John Sts. 506-453-2527. Closed Sat.-Sun. late Aug.–May),* with a freestanding spiral staircase.

Don't miss the lively indoor-outdoor **Boyce Farmers' Market★** *(Regent and George Sts. 506-451-1815. Sat. a.m.),* an institution older than the city. Highlights within Fredericton's busy calendar include the New Brunswick Summer Music Festival *(506-453-4697. Mid-Aug.),* the Mactaquac Craft Festival *(506-450-8989. Late Aug.–early Sept.),* the Fredericton Exhibition *(506-458-8819. Early Sept.),* and the Harvest Jazz & Blues Festival *(506-454-2583 Mid-Sept.).*

Head west on Trans-Canada 2 to scenic Hwy. 3 and meander south back to St. Stephen.

Kings Landing

Take a side trip to **Kings Landing Historical Settlement★★** *(21 mi/34 km W of Fredericton off Trans-Canada 2. 506-363-5090. June–mid-Oct.; adm. fee).* This exceptional living history museum re-creates the sights, sounds, and daily and seasonal rhythms of a 19th-century New Brunswick village. The restoration contains assorted historical structures spanning Loyalist to late Victorian times, brought to life by costumed interpreters demonstrating domestic and farm chores and trades, plus special events.

At Kings Landing Historical Settlement

Gaspé Peninsula★

● 650 miles/1,050 km ● 4 to 5 days ● Mid-May to mid-October

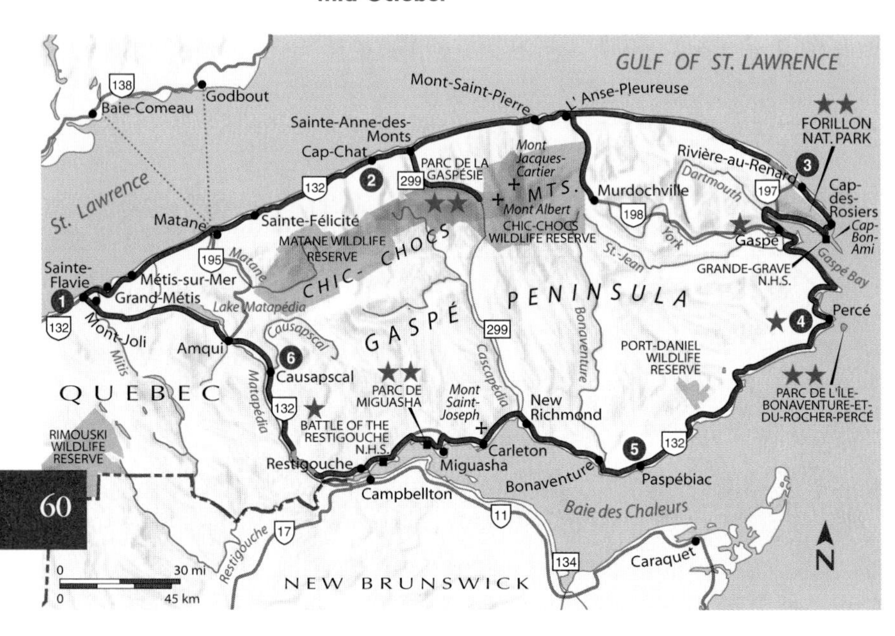

The name Gaspé is said to come from *gespeg*, the Mi'kmaq word for "land's end." Quebecers call it the *Gaspésie.* This remote and ruggedly beautiful peninsula is shaped by the sea and three cultures: Mi'kmaq, French, and British. A place of many moods and textures, defined by the fickle weather and light, the Gaspé is rich in art, history, and nature. This drive loops around the peninsula's hilly, rocky coast, wends through dense forest and centuries-old fishing villages, past picturesque farms and sparkling salmon streams, and enters the interior mountain fastness, where rise the majestic Chic-Chocs—the roof of Quebec.

By popular belief, the peninsula begins in the windy village of ❶ **Sainte-Flavie** *(Visitor Center 418-775-2223).* The widening St. Lawrence River laps just yards from the main Gaspé road, Hwy. 132, which forks here. Take the northern road and head through town—you can't miss the extraordinary sight of some 95 soulful, gray figures emerging from and floating on the sea. "Le Grand Rassemblement" ("the Great Gathering") is the inspired work of artist-writer Marcel Gagnol, whose workshop and gallery can be visited in the **Centre d'Art** *(Hwy. 132. 418-775-2829. Easter–mid-Oct.).*

Just up the road, the **Centre d'interprétation du Saumon atlantique (CISA)**★ *(Hwy. 132. 418-775-2969. Mid-May–mid-Oct.; adm. fee)* presents the story of the Atlantic salmon through aquarium exhibits, a film, live theater performances, and guided tours to the Mitis, a world-famous salmon river.

In **Grand-Métis** visit one of the world's most spectacular, intoxicating gardens, **Les Jardins de Métis**★★ *(Hwy. 132. 418-775-2221. June–mid-Oct.; adm. fee).* The 40-acre former estate of Elsie Reford is bursting with more than a thousand varieties nurtured by the humid microclimate. Her 37-room villa, built in 1887, is now a museum.

Salmon fishing along the Matane River

Drive up the coast where, in the late 1800s and early 1900s, wealthy Anglos from Montreal and Toronto claimed **Métis-sur-Mer** for their own. Their colony of sumptuous summer homes can be seen from the beach road.

Stay on Hwy. 132 east and proceed to the busy ferry-rail port of **Matane,** a major shrimp and salmon center where you see anglers casting for salmon right downtown in the shallow rapids of the Matane River, called Quebec's school for salmon fishing. A small exhibit area at **Mathieu-d'Amours Dam** *(260 av. Saint-Jérôme. 418-562-7006 (summer). June–mid-Oct.; adm. fee)* details the history of area bridges, dams, and fishing, with observation windows on a salmon ladder.

Beyond Sainte-Félicité, the landscape becomes more rugged, more intensely beautiful, as the road weaves to and from the coast, past rustic farmsteads, up into the forest. Stop at ❷ **Cap-Chat** to see **Éole** *(Off Hwy. 132. 418-786-5719. Late June–mid-Oct., guided tours only; adm. fee),* the world's tallest (equivalent to a 30-story building), most powerful vertical-axis wind turbine, named after the Greek god Aeolus. A thing of beauty in itself, it crowns the hill like a giant minimalist sculpture.

At **Sainte-Anne-des-Monts,** visit **Explorama★** *(1, 1re av. ouest. 418-763-2500. June–mid-Oct.; adm. fee),* an entertaining interpretive center featuring a colorful audiovisual exhibit on the Gaspé's regions and heritage, plus hands-on exhibits and experiments on marine science.

Éole wind turbine, Cap-Chat

For a change of scene, follow Rte. 299 south into the interior and **Parc de la Gaspésie★★** *(418-763-3301. Early June–mid-Oct.).* The drive is glorious, with awesome views of the forested Chic-Chocs (from the Mi'kmaq, *shickshocks*, or "rocky mountains"), the northern range in the Appalachian chain. This 310-square-mile park contains some of Quebec's highest peaks—4,160-foot Mont Jacques-Cartier and 3,554-foot Mont Albert, snowcapped until late summer and topped by tundra.

As you drive east on Hwy. 132 and round the top of the peninsula, the landscape becomes more remote, the settlements starker and more austere. A massive wall of rock forms the backdrop for the village of **Mont-Saint-Pierre,** where hang gliders from all over eastern Canada descend in summer. From L'Anse-Pleureuse, a few miles to the east, detour onto mountainous Hwy. 198 to the copper-mining town of **Murdochville,** which began as a company town in the early 1950s and bears the name of the mine's first president. Exhibits at the **Centre d'interprétation du cuivre★** *(Off Hwy. 198. 418-784-3335. Mid-May–mid-Oct., by appt. rest of year; adm. fee)* tell the region's mining story. Don a miner's helmet, light, and coveralls, and go underground to tour a preserved gallery mine drift. A full tour includes the nearby working mining complex.

Back on Hwy. 132, start around the Gaspé's hilly gulf shore to the fish-processing port of **3** **Rivière-au-Renard.** The **Centre d'interprétation des pêches contemporaines** *(1 Renard est. 418-269-5292. Mid-May–mid-Oct.; adm. fee)* provides an overview on the gulf fishing industry today. From here Hwy. 132 runs through **Forillon National Park★★** *(418-368-5505. Park open year-round, Interpretation Centre*

The Gaspé Road

Prior to 1929 no road circumvented the isolated Gaspé peninsula. Before 1925, horse carts were used as transportation from Matane, but beyond Sainte-Anne-des-Monts even the paths were unreliable. In addition, some spots were impassable without a boat. All that changed in 1929 with the extension of boulevard Perron to Cap-des-Rosiers, completing the circuit and paving the way for tourism. But it was no picnic. Unpaved, with blind turns, abrupt drop-offs, bottomless gorges, and flooding, the road itself was an adventure. A 1933 visitors' guide advised drivers "to be all eyes, all ears...to never exceed 30 miles per hour...and always keep to the right...." Not until the fifties did serious road improvements begin.

June–mid-Oct.; adm. fee), where the Appalachians meet the Gulf of St. Lawrence. At **Cap-des-Rosiers** (named by Samuel de Champlain for the rampant wild roses), enter the park's North Sector. A monument along the breakwater commemorates the Irish immigrants who shipwrecked off the treacherous coast in 1847. (Many of the survivors were taken in by local families, accounting for the Irish blood around these parts.) At the interpretation center, aquariums, hands-on exhibits, and a short walk introduce the park's theme: The Harmony between Man, Land, and Sea. Head out to spectacular **Cap-Bon-Ami,** home to colonies of seals and seabirds, where stairs descend to the beach, sheltered beneath a magnificent tangle of roots and mossy rocks, soaring conifers and delicate cascades, and massive and ancient sedimentary outcroppings. Drive along an astonishingly beautiful stretch of Hwy. 132, and continue into the park's South Sector to **Grande-Grave National Historic Site.** Once an important fishing center, it is now marked by 26 restored buildings.

Wind around Gaspé Bay to the historic fishing and mining center of **Gaspé★.** The city overlooks a generous natural harbor into which flow three fine salmon rivers. In 1534 Jacques Cartier planted a cross somewhere in the vicinity, claiming the territory for France. The **Musée de la Gaspésie★** *(80 boul. Gaspé. 418-368-1534. Adm. fee)* celebrates the region's unique heritage and culture, from prehistory through the present. The evocative stelae standing nearby comprise the **Jacques Cartier Monument National Historic Site,** commemorating this first official act in Canadian history. Nearby, an interpretive trail traces the shore.

After some 45 miles (74 km), Hwy. 132 descends steeply into busy **4 Percé★** *(Visitor Center 418-782-5448. Late May–Oct.).* Here you are face-to-face with the Gaspé's most famous landmarks: Percé Rock and Bonaventure Island, centerpieces of the **Parc de l'Île-Bonaventure-et-du-Rocher-Percé★★** *(Interpretation*

Forillon National Park, Gulf of St. Lawrence

Centre, Rang de l'Irlande. 418-782-2721. June–mid-Oct.; fare for boat tours and ferries). At low tide, walk out to the limestone monolith *(path from rue Mont-Joli).* The interpretation center features exhibits on the gulf's diverse life zones and a fascinating, short video on the island's northern gannet colony, numbering about 64,000 (out of about 168,000 seabirds total) in summer. If the fog has socked in, Percé offers many rainy-day diversions, including **Musée le Chafaud** *(Hwy. 132. 418-782-5100. June–Sept.; adm. fee),* showcasing traditional and contemporary art.

Continue on to the beautiful Baie des Chaleurs ("Bay of Heat"), and stop in at ❺ **Paspébiac,** one of the Gaspé's first permanent fishing posts. You can see the original structures built by the big British fishing monopolies at the **Site historique du Banc-de-Paspébiac** *(Rte. du Quai. 418-752-6229. Mid-June–mid-Oct.; adm. fee),* as well as observe demonstrations of traditional trades. Go on to **Bonaventure,** founded by exiled Acadian farmers in 1760, and a fitting locale for the **Musée acadien du Québec**★ *(95 av. Port-Royal. 418-534-4000. Adm. fee).* The poignant story of Quebec's Acadians is beautifully told in this museum of history and ethnology.

To the west, in the former loyalist stronghold of **New Richmond,** stands the **Gaspesian British Heritage Centre** *(351 boul. Perron ouest. 418-392-4487. Mid-June–Labor Day; adm. fee).* This historic village, consisting of some 20 structures staffed by costumed interpreters, celebrates the diverse cultural contributions made by Scottish, Irish, English, and Channel Island immigrants.

Percé Rock, Parc de l'Île-Bonaventure-et-du-Rocher-Percé

A long, narrow sandbar, or *barachois,* marks **Carleton,** an Acadian community and resort town nestled beneath Mont Saint-Joseph. Herons, terns, and others frequent the bird sanctuary out on the point. Above all presides the mountaintop **Shrine of Notre Dame of Mont Saint-Joseph,** offering panoramic views of the town, the bay below, and New Brunswick beyond. A little gem, this unique church

Former cod dealer's base, Site historique du Banc-de-Paspébiac

within a church contains a sublime altar mosaic and a crèche made of a beachcomber's treasures.

About 9 miles (14 km) farther on Hwy. 132, turn off to **Parc de Miguasha★★** *(Rte. Miguasha ouest. 418-794-2475. June–mid-Oct.).* The fossiliferous cliff along the Restigouche River estuary reads like a field guide on the Devonian Period (410 to 360 million years ago). One of the world's richest sites, it is remarkable for the quality, quantity, and biodiversity of its fossil fauna and flora. The tour includes interpretive center exhibits, the laboratory, and a cliff walk.

Take Hwy. 132 on to the **Battle of the Restigouche National Historic Site★** *(418-788-5676. June–mid-Oct.; adm. fee).* In 1760 the fate of New France was sealed offshore during this naval battle. On hand are an impressive collection of artifacts, including a barrel of petrified salt pork, and authentic ship timbers retrieved from the sunken French frigate. An excellent video recounts the event.

The last leg of the drive wends through the emerald valley of the Matapédia River, where signs of human life are few, save for the odd angler wading in this famous salmon river. A conical, smoke-belching chimney casts a faint blue haze over ❻ **Causapscal,** filling the air with the nostalgic smell of wood smoke. **Matamajaw Historic Site** *(53 rue St.-Jacques sud. 418-756-5999. June-Sept.; adm. fee)* preserves the site of the exclusive Matamajaw Salmon Club, founded here in the early 1900s. On the banks of the Causapscal River, watch salmon jumping in the pool at **Les Chutes et le Marais,** and stroll the nature trails. Then continue on Hwy. 132 back to Sainte-Flavie.

St. Lawrence Circuit★

● 420 miles/675 km ● 4 to 5 days ● Mid-May through October

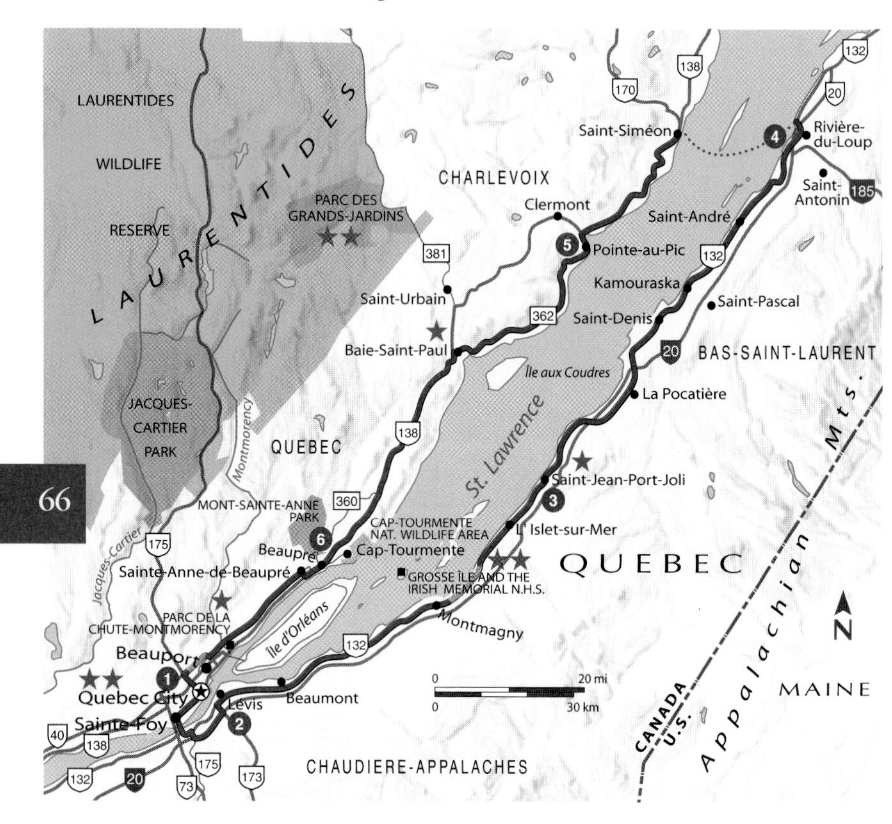

This loop drive takes you along both shores of the magnificent St. Lawrence River. Start in the walled capital of Quebec City—the closest you'll get to Old Europe this side of the Atlantic—then drive the south shore route as it marries the gentle, rolling foothills and farms of the Chaudière-Appalaches region with the more rocky and rugged coast of the Bas-Saint-Laurent. Complete the loop by ferrying to the north shore and heading upriver, through the gorgeous hill country of the Charlevoix.

Begin with the walled city, the heart and soul of French Canada (and a UNESCO world heritage site), ❶ **Quebec City**★★ *(Visitor Center, 60 rue d'Auteuil. 418-692-2471).* The main attraction is **Vieux-Québec**★★—Old Quebec City. Quebecois clearly love their old city, which climbs in tiers above the St. Lawrence, from the waterside **Lower Town,** or Basse-Ville, to the stone-walled **Upper Town,** or Haute-Ville. On a fine day, life spills into the streets, lined with sidewalk cafés and pulsing with people. Enter via **Grande Allée,** the Champs-Élysées of Quebec, through **Porte Saint-Louis,** one of the four gates to the Old City.

Quebec's history hits you at every turn. In 1608 explorer Samuel de Champlain founded a small fur-trading post here, on the site of what would become the capital of New France. The French fortified their city, but in 1759 it fell to the British, a defeat that all but ended France's military presence in Canada. **Québec Expérience** *(8 rue du Trésor. 418-694-4000. Adm. fee),* a multimedia spectacle, covers 400 years of the city's history. Review Quebec's military past at the **Musée du Fort** *(10 rue Ste.-Anne. 418-692-2175. Adm. fee).*

Next, head for the **Citadel National Historic Site★★** *(Côte de la Citadelle. 418-694-2815. May-Oct.; adm. fee),* Quebec's east-flank fortification atop Cap Diamant. The massive star-shaped Citadel contains 25 buildings that span two centuries, with military exhibits at the **Museum of the Royal 22nd Regiment.** A golden-horned goat, a copy of a gift from Queen Victoria, accompanies the elaborate Changing of the Guard *(mid-June–Labor Day).*

Old Port, Lower Town, Quebec City

Below sprawl the historical **Plains of Abraham.** Bloodied during the decisive battles of the mid-1700s, they are now the peaceful site of **Parc des Champs-de-Bataille★** (Battlefields Park), a popular urban refuge. Here, the **Musée du Québec★★** *(Entrance on Grande Allée. 418-643-2150. Closed Mon. Sept.-May; adm. fee)* showcases artwork ranging from ancient to contemporary times. In the old city prison, part of the museum complex, the **National Battlefields Park Interpretation Center** *(418-648-5641. Closed Mon. Labor Day–mid-May)* presents a multimedia exhibit *(fee)* on the history of the Plains. From the

Citadel, follow the **Promenade des Gouverneurs★** to **Terrasse Dufferin,** a panoramic boardwalk alongside the multiturreted **Château Frontenac** *(418-692-3861),* a landmark grand hotel completed in 1893.

The walls themselves, more formally known as **Fortifications of Quebec National Historic Site★★** *(Visitor Center in Esplanade Powder Magazine, 100 rue St.-Louis. 418-648-7016. April-Oct.; adm. fee),* represent 300 years of military engineering. You haven't seen Quebec until you've traipsed at least a part of the nearly 3-mile-long defense system along **rue des Remparts.**

Royal 22nd Regiment at Château Frontenac

Explore the Old City's labyrinth of steep narrow streets *(self-guided walking tour info. available at Visitor Center),* where the Upper Town offers a sidewalk art gallery on **rue du Trésor,** and the exquisite **Chapelle des Ursulines** *(12 rue Donnacona).* Adjacent is the **Musée des Ursulines de Québec** *(418-694-0694. Closed Mon.; adm. fee),* which contains everyday artifacts and relics. The **Musée des Augustines** *(32 rue Charlevoix. 418-692-2492. Closed Mon.)* displays an eclectic collection of art and *objets,* including 17th-century medical instruments.

Take the Escalier Casse-Cou ("breakneck stairs") to the Lower Town. In lively **Quartier du Petit-Champlain★★,** a restored 1700s-1800s village, choose an outdoor café and watch the passing parade. Still older **Place-Royale★★,** site of Champlain's trading post, holds a wealth of 17th- and 18th-century architecture, notably the 1688 **Église Notre-Dame-des-Victoires.** Don't miss the exciting **Musée de la Civilisation★★** *(85 rue Dalhousie. 418-643-2158. Closed Mon. Labor Day–mid-June; adm. fee),* which offers at least ten thematic exhibits—three permanent, all state of the art—on the human experience. Then browse the antique shops along **rue Saint-Paul** opposite the **Vieux-Port★** ("old port"), where the colorful **Marché du Vieux-Port,** the market, sells the sweetest strawberries.

Depart Quebec City and cross the river to ❷ **Lévis** and **Fort No. 1 at Pointe-de-Lévy National Historic Site** *(Off Hwy. 132 at 41 chemin du Gouvernement. 418-835-5182. Daily mid-May–Aug., Sept.-Oct. Sun. only; adm. fee).* One of five 19th-century forts built by the British at Pointe-de-Lévy,

No. 1 occupies a promontory higher than the Citadel and is unique for its shape and innovative engineering.

Continue on Hwy. 132 to **Beaumont** and **Le Moulin de Beaumont** *(2 rue du Fleuve. 418-833-1867. Call for hours; adm. fee),* an 1821 mill that still turns out whole-wheat flour on buhrstones. A perfect picnic stop, bring your own makings or find something here. As the rolling fields and pastures of the Chaudière-Appalaches give way to an increasingly rocky landscape, the mood changes as often as the weather (the mercurial St. Lawrence generates its own meteorological system).

After some 25 miles (40 km), you'll reach **Montmagny,** port for **Grosse Île and the Irish Memorial National Historic Site★★** *(Park office, 2 rue d'Auteuil. 418-563-4009. May-Oct.; adm. fee).* Canada's Ellis Island, Grosse Île served as a quarantine station for more than four million European immigrants, most of them Irish, from 1832 to 1937. The site preserves at least 30 buildings and monuments. Each spring and fall, this area is also a stopover for thousands of migrating greater snow geese. The **Migration Education Center★** *(53 rue du Bassin Nord. 418-248-4565. May-Nov.; adm. fee)* presents the story of both these important migrations, including a poignant video show about the Irish of Grosse Île.

Up the road, the village of **L'Islet-sur-Mer,** home port of many captains and seamen, celebrates the St. Lawrence maritime heritage at **Musée Maritime Bernier** *(Hwy. 132. 418-247-5001. Closed weekends mid-Oct.–mid-May; adm. fee).* Along with exhibits of nautical artifacts and a children's

Île d'Orléans

Tired of city touring? This slow-paced, bucolic island—Quebec's largest historic district—offers a quick reprieve just 15 minutes northeast of Quebec City. The 42-mile (68 km) circular road leads past fields farmed by 15 generations, through six charming villages sprinkled with old churches, manor houses, and mills. Pick your own strawberries in July and apples in the fall. For information on historic sites, museums, galleries, wineries, farms, and restaurants, stop by the tourist office *(195 chemin Royale. 418-828-9411).*

Along Hwy. 132, paralleling the St. Lawrence River

area, the museum keeps a Canadian Coast Guard icebreaker and a hydrofoil warship docked out back.

You know you're in ❸ **Saint-Jean-Port-Joli★** by the rampant wood-carvers' studios. In June the place teems with artists, mostly sculptors, during the annual Fête Internationale de la Sculpture. Visit the **Maison Médard Bourgault★** *(Hwy. 132. 418-598-3880. Mid-June–Labor Day; adm. fee),* home of Saint-Jean-Port-Joli's master sculptor (1897-1967), whose imaginative carvings decorate the walls and furniture. Next door, the **Musée des anciens canadiens★** *(Hwy. 132. 418-598-3392. Mid-May–mid-Oct.; adm. fee)* displays carvings by known and new artists.

The land turns noticeably more hilly as you enter the Bas-Saint-Laurent region at La Pocatière. Near Kamouraska rocky mounds interrupt the flat, green fields. Continue northeast on Hwy. 132 to the bluff city of ❹ **Rivière-du-Loup** *(Visitor Center, 189 rue Hôtel-de-Ville. 418-867-3015),* overlooking the Îles du Bas-Saint-Laurent—"lower St. Lawrence islands." The railroad made this a hub in the late 1800s and it's still a crossroads. A self-guided walking tour *(brochure available at Visitor Center)* reveals the town's architectural heritage. Regional art and ethnology are the featured themes at the small **Musée du Bas-Saint-Laurent** *(300 rue St.-Pierre. 418-862-7547. Adm. fee).*

From here, take the ferry *(Rivière-du-Loup/St.-Siméon Ferry, dock on rue Hayward. 418-862-5094. Call for schedule and arrive early; fare)* to the glorious Charlevoix region on the north shore. The Charlevoix is part of the Canadian Shield, an ancient geological formation, and characterized by glacial peaks and valleys, gentle shores, rocky palisades, unusual flora and fauna, and quaint villages—the whole region was declared a UNESCO world biosphere reserve for its unique mix of nature and culture.

From the landing, drive southwest on Hwy. 138, bearing off onto Rte. 362 for ❺ **Pointe-au-Pic,** a turn-of-the-century summer spot for the social elite. Drive down the **chemin des Falaises** to see their handsome, bluff-top mansions, many now converted to inns. Grandest of all is the **Manoir Richelieu** *(181 rue Richelieu. 418-665-3703 or 800-463-2613),* a resort hotel and casino. The **Galérie d'Art Au**

Great Gardens

As a side trip, head for the hills to unique **Parc des Grands-Jardins★★** (Visitor Center about 20 mi/32 km N of Baie-Saint-Paul via Rte. 381. 418-457-3945. Late May–Oct.). A major part of the central biosphere reserve, the 120-square-mile park is an anomalous islet of Quebec's far north. Its distinguishing feature, the taiga, is a nordic wonderland of spongy lichen, black spruce, and miniature flowers, inhabited by caribou, and accessible by an easy, well-marked walking trail.

Musée Maritime Bernier, L'Islet-sur-Mer

P'tit Bonheur *(Rte. 362/Blvd. Bellevue. 418-665-2060. Closed Mon.-Fri. Nov.-Feb.)* features Quebec artists, while the **Musée de Charlevoix★** *(1 chemin du Havre. 418-665-4411. Closed Mon. Labor Day–late June; adm. fee)* presents diverse exhibits on regional history, ethnology, and art. Proceed to **Baie-Saint-Paul★,** an enchanting artist community and one of Quebec's oldest towns. Here, the architecturally acclaimed **Centre d'Exposition★** *(23 rue Ambroise-Fafard. 418-435-3681. Adm. fee)* exhibits contemporary work in airy galleries, while the **Centre d'Art★** *(4 rue Ambroise-Fafard. 418-435-3681. Visitor info. also available)* showcases Charlevoix artists.

Parc des Grands-Jardins, north of Baie-Saint-Paul

Next, head southwest on Hwy. 138 to 6 **Beaupré** and the **Grand Canyon des Chutes Sainte-Anne** *(Off Hwy. 138. 418-827-4057. May-Oct.; adm. fee),* where a nature walk leads across three suspension bridges slung dramatically over the rocky gorge, with a bird's-eye view of the stunning Sainte-Anne Falls. Nearby, visit **Cap Tourmente National Wildlife Area** *(St.-Joachim-de-Montmorency. 418-827-4591. Adm. fee seasonal),* where tens of thousands of greater snow geese descend in spring and fall.

To the west, in **Sainte-Anne-de-Beaupré,** is the **Basilique Sainte-Anne-de-Beaupré** *(10018 av. Royale. 418-827-3781),* a magnificent, medieval-style cathedral containing some 200 stained-glass windows. From here, follow avenue Royale, which parallels Hwy. 138 but is centuries distant. This old country road promises a mix of traditional architecture and rural vignettes en route to **Parc de la Chute-Montmorency★** *(2490 av. Royale, Beauport. 418-663-2877. Adm. fee).* Its centerpiece is a 272-foot-high waterfall (about 100 feet higher than Niagara Falls). Ride the gondola *(fare)* for an impressive aerial view, or get a closer look from the footbridge and stairway. At the top of the falls, visit the interpretation center at **Manoir Montmorency.**

Montreal Area★★

● 385 miles/620 km ● 5 to 6 days ● Mid-May through October

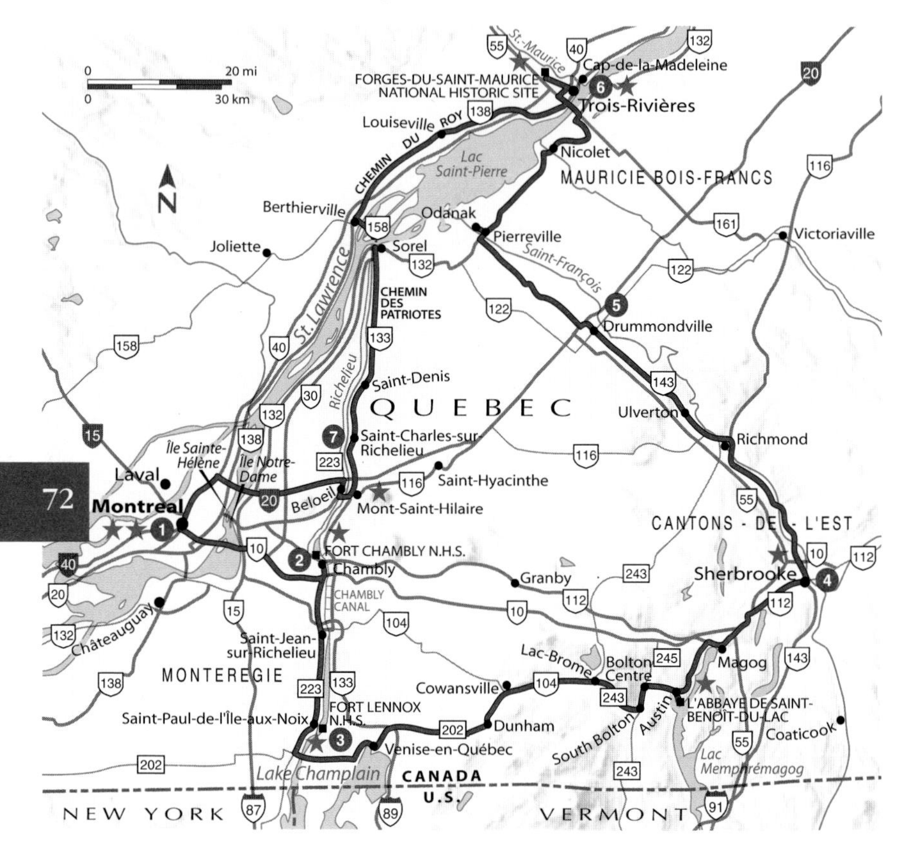

Like a good French wine, this drive offers a complex blend of history, culture, and scenery. Begin in Montreal, one of the world's largest French-speaking cities with more museums, cultural events, restaurants, and shops than you can count. Then head out into "the regions" (anyplace outside the city on this route), first southeast through pastoral Montérégie, then rolling through the British-settled Eastern Townships, and Quebec's picturesque wine country, crossing into the Mauricie Bois-Francs region and over the St. Lawrence River. Complete the loop along two historic river roads, le chemin du Roy, which traces the St. Lawrence, and le chemin des Patriotes, which follows the Richelieu.

Montrealers understand paradox. Theirs is a city at once northern and Latin, sophisticated and provincial, and conversant in two languages. Whatever your vantage point,

❶ **Montreal★★** *(Centre Infotouriste 514-873-2015 or 800-363-7777)* promises something different.

First explored in 1535 by Jacques Cartier, the city was founded as a missionary colony in 1642 by Paul de Chomedey de Maisonneuve. Today, its French flair is irrepressible and irresistible. The most dramatic entrée to the island of Montreal—largest in the Hochelaga Archipelago, of which the city of Montreal occupies one third—is via Pont Champlain. At dusk, the skyline soars and glitters against silhouetted Mont-Royal. This generally walkable city (although the Metro, Montreal's subway, is user friendly) can be divided into five sections. The first, named Mont-Royal by Cartier, and known as "the mountain," offers lovely **Parc du Mont-Royal★,** designed by Frederick Law Olmsted. A pilgrimage site, the magnificent **Oratoire Saint-Joseph** *(3800 chemin Queen Mary. 514-733-8211)* boasts a massive copper dome and lofty views.

Downtown caters to every taste, from the trendy **Quartier Latin★** centered around rue Saint-Denis, to elegant rue Sherbrooke, where the **Musée des beaux-arts de**

Montreal skyline above the Vieux-Port

Montréal★★ *(1379-80 rue Sherbrooke ouest. 514-285-1600. Closed Mon.; adm. fee)* displays a world-class collection of historic and contemporary Canadian and international art, with fine temporary exhibits. Near the McGill University campus, the **Musée McCord d'histoire canadienne★** *(690 rue Sherbrooke ouest. 514-398-7100. Closed Mon.; adm.*

fee) features exhibits on ethnology, archaeology, costumes and textiles, decorative arts, and cultural heritage. Also worthwhile is the **Canadian Center for Architecture★** *(1920 rue Baile. 514-939-7026. May-Sept. Tues.-Sun., Oct.-April Wed.-Sun.; adm. fee),* a preeminent museum dedicated to international architecture, and the **Musée d'art contemporain de Montréal★★** *(185 rue Ste.-Catherine ouest. 514-847-6212. Closed Mon.; adm. fee),* a showcase of post-1940 art adjoining the **Place des Arts** *(175 rue Ste.-Catherine ouest. 514-842-2112),* the performing arts complex.

Musée des beaux-arts de Montréal

As if there weren't enough to see at street level, the **Underground City★** offers some 18 miles of seamlessly linked pedestrian malls. If you feel a bit like Alice among the queen's hedgerows, stop at one of the strategically located information kiosks.

The narrow, cobbled streets and solid, centuries-old buildings of **Vieux-Montréal★★,** the once fortified old city, offer endless amusement. A lively nightspot, by day its galleries, boutiques, and historic sites entice. Take a peek at the magnificent polychromatic interior and stained-glass windows of **Notre-Dame Basilica★** *(110 rue Notre-Dame ouest. 514-842-2925),* constructed in 1829. The colorful **Vieux-Port** harbors historic **Chapelle Notre-Dame-de-Bon-secours** *(400 rue St.-Paul est),* where sailors prayed before setting to sea. Don't miss the **Pointe-à-Callière, Montreal Archaeology and History Museum★★** *(350 place Royale. 514-872-9134. Closed Mon.; adm. fee),* built on the actual site where the city was founded in 1642. It features a multimedia show on Montreal's history and a subterranean tour of layered ruins dating from the 1600s, plus displays of artifacts, interactive virtual figures, an archaeological crypt, and exhibits in the old Custom House.

In the east-end area of Maisonneuve, visit **Olympic Park★** *(4141 av. Pierre-de-Coubertin. 514-252-8687. Adm. fee to some sites),* which includes the 1976 Olympic stadium and boasts the world's tallest inclined tower. The former cycling track has been ingeniously converted to the **Biodôme de Montréal★★** *(4777 av. Pierre-de-Coubertin. 514-868-3000. Adm. fee),* a unique environmental museum that re-creates four distinct ecosystems, from a sticky tropical forest to the chilly poles. Here you can see small animals in their own habitats, including a bat cave, a beaver dam, and free-range birds. Nearby, the spectacular, 185-acre **Jardin Botanique de Montréal★★** *(4101 rue Sherbrooke est. 514-872-1400. Adm. fee)* contains about 30 outdoor gardens, notably the Chinese and Japanese, and the rose garden. The indoor Insectarium houses some 150,000 live and mounted insects, plus hands-on exhibits, a butterfly house (in summer), and a fascinating film about an insect hunter. You might even stumble upon an insect-tasting of barbecued bugs dipped in maple syrup.

The islands, Île Notre-Dame and Île Sainte-Hélène, comprise the vast, green **Parc-des-Îles.** The former, man-made for Expo 67, claims the **Casino de Montréal** *(1 av. du Casino. 514-392-2746)* in the old French and Quebec pavilions, while the latter hosts the **Biosphere** *(160 chemin Tour-de-l'Îsle. 514-283-5000. Daily in summer, Sept.–early June Tues.-Sat.; adm. fee),* the American pavilion's giant geodesic dome, now Canada's first ecowatch center.

Notre-Dame Basilica, Montreal

To leave Montreal, follow Hwy. 10 east across Pont Champlain. The flat, open plains of the Montérégie region soon replace the urban congestion. Exit at ❷ **Chambly** and drive through town to watch the keepers manually operate the old locks at historic **Chambly Canal** *(1840 rue Bourgogne. 514-658-0681. Call for hours and events),* inaugurated in 1843 as a shipping link between Chambly and Saint-Jean-sur-Richelieu. Nearby, **Fort Chambly National Historic Site★** *(2 rue Richelieu. 514-658-1585. Call for hours and special summer events; adm. fee),* overlooking the Chambly Basin, preserves the site of a 1665 French stockade, replaced in 1709 by this stone fortification, which the British then took in 1760. Exhibits provide background for a self-guided tour of the fort, restored to the 1750s.

Proceed south on Rte. 223 through the flat Richelieu Valley, noting signs of seigneurial influence in the region's planning and architecture. For example, the way the fields are planted at odd angles is a legacy of the old French colonial system, in which the land was partitioned in narrow strips always perpendicular to the waterways.

Just beyond **Saint-Paul-de-l'Île-aux-Noix** is the British fortification at ❸ **Fort Lennox National Historic Site**★ *(1 av. 61e, off Rte. 223. 514-291-5700. Daily mid-May–Aug., weekends Sept.–mid-Oct.; adm. fee).* A ferry transports you to **l'Île-aux-Noix,** the small island on which the fort stands. Along with the well-preserved fortifications, you'll find a restaurant and a picnic area. Pick up Rte. 202, **la Route des Vignobles** ("the vintners' trail"), along the U.S. border through Quebec's rolling wine country, known for its white Seyval *(wine-tour brochure and map available locally).*

Lake Champlain appears suddenly in all its glory near **Venise-en-Québec,** a modest summer resort that in no way resembles its eponym. The road winds around the lake's north shore before veering northeast into the Eastern Townships, or les Cantons-de-l'est, region. Look south for a breathtaking view of the Vermont and New York lakeshores, and the Adirondack Mountains.

To the east lies the heart of wine country, **Dunham,** a quaint village blessed with beautiful forested plains, a backdrop of Appalachian peaks—and a microclimate that produces excellent apples as well as grapes.

Find your way to Rte. 245 and Bolton Centre, detour-

Abbaye de Saint-Benoît-du-Lac

ing toward Austin and following the signs to the **Abbaye de Saint-Benoît-du-Lac**★ *(819-843-4080. Call for service times).* Magnificently situated above Lac Memphrémagog, the Benedictine abbey's grounds offer a soothing time-out. Their acclaimed choir recites prayers in Gregorian chant. Recordings, abbey-made cheese, and other items are sold in the shop *(closed Sun.).*

Next, head north to Magog via beautiful chemin Nicholas-Austin and catch Hwy. 112 east to ❹ **Sherbrooke★** *(Tourist Office 819-564-8331 or 800-561-8331),* the regional capital of the Eastern Townships. For an introduction to the history of Sherbrooke and the townships, begin with the **Centre d'interprétation de l'histoire de Sherbrooke** *(275 rue Dufferin. 819-821-5406. Closed Mon.; adm. fee).* From here, take the self-guided walking tour through the historic Old North neighborhood. Next door to the center, the **Musée des beaux-arts de Sherbrooke** *(241 rue Dufferin. 819-821-2115. Closed Mon.; adm. fee)* exhibits historic and contemporary work by regional artists, "naive" art, and a variety of changing shows. The theme is natural history at the **Musée du Séminaire de Sherbrooke** *(222 rue Frontenac. 819-564-3200. Closed Mon. Sept.–mid-June; adm. fee),* known for its unusual displays and hands-on exhibits.

Dairy farm, near Ulverton

Down in the Magog River Gorge, **Centrale Frontenac** *(Rue Frontenac. 819-821-5406. Late June–Labor Day Wed.-Sun.; adm. fee),* Quebec's oldest operating hydroelectric plant, offers interactive exhibits and guided tours. For a closer look, walk along the interpretive **Magog River Trail.**

Drive north along the sometimes elusive Hwy. 143, which parallels the river and the train tracks, a legacy of Sherbrooke's glory days as a 19th-century rail hub. Notice the British influence here in the town names and the distinctive architecture. At Ulverton, you are in the Mauricie Bois-Francs region. Visit a restored 19th-century woolen mill, **Moulin à laine d'Ulverton** *(212 chemin Porter. 819-826-3157. June–mid-Oct., call for hours; adm. fee),* which contains a complete set of original, working machinery, with demonstrations and related exhibits.

Press on to ❺ **Drummondville** and **Le village québécois d'Antan★★** *(Off Hwy. 122, E on rue Montplaisir. 819-478-1441. June–Labor Day. Adm. fee).* This delightful, open-air museum convincingly re-creates a rural Quebec

Le village québécois d'Antan

village during the century of townships settlement. Period-dressed interpreters bring to life the settlers' world, demonstrating their crafts and daily tasks among 70 renovated and reconstructed buildings and a working farm. Sample the cheese, bread, and molasses cookies made on site.

Hwy. 143 leads northwest, where the land levels out again and the air is grassy sweet. Take Hwy. 132 into the Wabanaki (Abenaki is the French spelling) Reserve at **Odanak,** a Wabanaki homeland since the mid-1600s. The small **Musée des Abenakis** *(514-568-2600. Closed weekends Nov.-April; adm. fee)* displays artifacts and crafts. There are also several souvenir shops in the community.

Hwy. 55 travels across the St. Lawrence to ❻ **Trois-Rivières★** *(Tourist Office, 1563 rue Notre-Dame. 819-375-1122. Closed weekends Oct.-May, info. on self-guided theme walks available),* capital of the Mauricie Bois-Francs region and Quebec's second oldest city, founded in 1634. The name refers to the three channels branching the mouth of the St. Maurice River. Trois-Rivières begs a pedestrian's pace. Start at the **Musée des arts et traditions populaires du Québec★★** *(200 rue Laviolette. 819-372-0406. Closed Mon. Sept.–late June; adm. fee)* for a colorful overview of Quebec life, from prehistoric times to the present, and a wonderful folk art display. Exhibits in the adjoining 1822 prison paint a riveting picture of life behind these walls. The heart of the old city, **rue des Ursulines★★,** is a preserve of 18th-century landmarks, including **Saint-James Church,** the **Maison Hertel de la Fresnière,** and the **Musée des Ursulines** *(734 rue des Ursulines. 819-375-7922. Closed Oct., call for hours; adm. fee),* which encompasses an eclectic collection of glass-cased shrines and religious objects, plus the decorative chapel and refectory exhibits. Promenade along the inviting waterfront and visit the big, splashy **Centre d'exposition sur l'industries des pâtes et papiers★** *(800 Parc portuaire. 819-372-4633. May-Sept.; adm. fee)* for a comprehensive look at Quebec's pulp-and-paper industry, of which Trois-Rivières forms the center.

Take a side trip to the **Forges-du-Saint-Maurice National Historic Site★** *(10000 boul. des Forges. 819-378-5116. May-Oct.; adm. fee),* Canada's first ironworks,

Gibelotte

Sorel's regional dish—you won't find it anywhere else—came from Berthe Beauchemin's kitchen in the 1920s. Traditionally, the thick fish and vegetable soup called gibelotte is served with bread, butter, and onions, complemented with a plate of roasted perch and a bottle of wine. Several places offer it, but for a true cultural experience, drive to **Restaurant Chez Marc Beauchemin** *(124 Île d'Embarras. 514-743-6023. Bring your own wine)*, the home of gibelotte, where they serve it up, *sans façon*—family-style, in a canalside shack.

founded in 1730 and in operation for 150 years. Along with exhibits on forge history in the old blast furnace, an interpretive path guides you around the site.

Drive west along the breathtaking expanse of Lac Saint-Pierre on historic Hwy. 138—**le chemin du Roy** ("the king's way"), Canada's first viable road, opened in 1737. Only the passing commercial boat illustrates that this so-called lake is actually a widening of the St. Lawrence. Take Hwy. 158 east to its end, where a ferry *(no reservations; fare)* delivers you to the shores of pleasant **Sorel** *(Tourist Office, 92 chemin des Patriotes. 514-746-9441)*. The giant grain elevators are a sure sign you're back in the bountiful Montérégie. Wander the historic district *(self-guided tour info. available at Tourist Office)* to visit the old town market *(Wed.-Sat.)*, and the mosaicked, 1822 **Église Saint-Pierre de Sorel** *(170 rue George. Sat.-Sun.)*.

Trois-Rivières café along the St. Lawrence River

The last leg of the drive, Hwy. 133, follows the Richelieu River along a beautiful, historic corridor known as **le chemin des Patriotes,** named for the nearby clash of Patriot and British troops during the Patriots Rebellion of the mid-1830s. Watch for fabulous examples of traditional Quebec architecture. Drive through the bucolic Montérégie countryside to another charming community, ❼ **Saint-Charles-sur-Richelieu.** Stop at the lovely old stone church at the edge of the village; the cemetery is a work of art, with stark white statuary forming the Stations of the Cross against a backdrop of fields and the mountain of Mont-Saint-Hilaire.

At the foot of the mountain awaits the enchanting artist colony of **Mont-Saint-Hilaire★.** The **Centre de conservation de la nature du Mont-Saint-Hilaire** *(422 chemin des Moulins. 514-467-1755. Adm. fee)*, a UNESCO biosphere reserve, contains a magnificent nature park.

Take Hwy. 116 west, across the river, to **Beloeil,** a quiet village with a charming old quarter and a stunning view of the mountain. From this tranquil reprieve, Trans-Canada 20 leads back toward the bright lights of Montreal.

Capital Region★★

● 350 miles/560 km ● 3 to 5 days ● Spring, summer, fall (and winter for the dauntless)

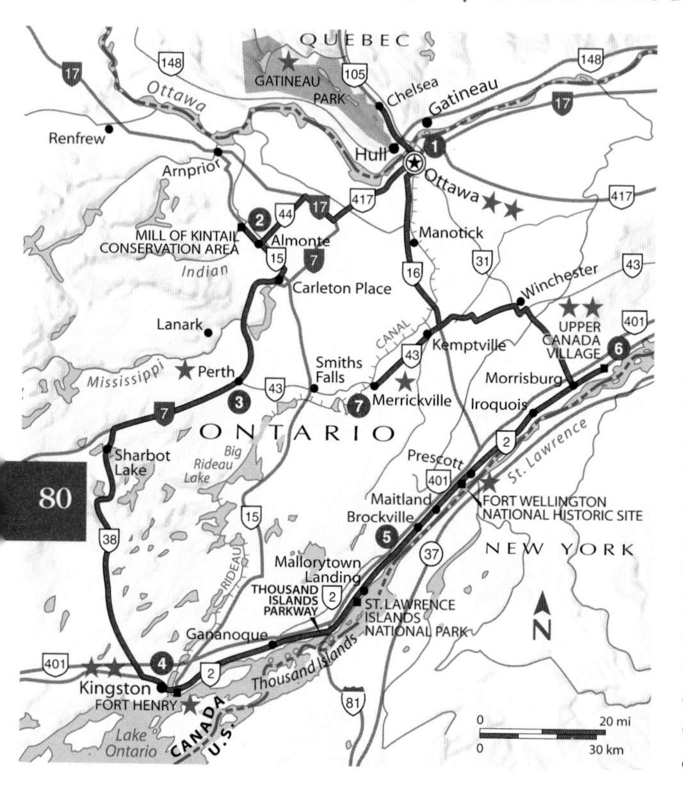

Comparatively, eastern Ontario may lack southwestern Ontario's industry, easily arable soil, and wealth, but it more than compensates with history, geographical and human character, and a flinty refusal to be other than itself. This tour begins in Ottawa, a culturally rich and eminently negotiable capital city. From there it proceeds through one of the southernmost outcroppings of the Canadian Shield, down to charming Kingston, and along the St. Lawrence River. After a visit to a superb historical re-creation, it's north again, stopping off at Merrickville on the Rideau Canal, and back to Ottawa.

At times self-deprecation seems like the Canadian national sport, nowhere more so than when it comes to the national capital. But ❶ **Ottawa★★** *(Ottawa Tourism 613-237-5150 or 800-363-4465),* one of the world's most delightful as well as manageable capitals, needs no apologies. Bisected by the Rideau Canal, Ottawa softens the gray stone of its public buildings with parks, gardens, and a flourishing daily farmers' market in the center of town. Called the **By Ward Market** *(George, Sussex, St. Patrick, and Cumberland Sts. 613-562-3325),* it's full of interesting shops and cafés.

The logical starting place for visitors is **Parliament Hill★★** *(613-992-4793),* a superb meld of neo-Gothic urbanity built in the 1860s and '70s. Most glorious of all is the Library of Parliament, its 16 sides bristling with flying buttresses and its inside an almost folkloric piece of Gothic Revival extravaganza. Tours offering an introduction to Canada's political system as well as to the buildings are available daily. Those with a taste for military ritual will find it on the East Lawn every summer morning *(mid-June–mid-Aug. 10 a.m.),* when, accompanied by a military band, the **Changing the Guard Ceremony** takes place, with both the Governor General's Foot Guards and the Canadian Grenadier Guards in attendance.

When it comes to museums, the Ottawa area is an embarrassment of riches. Two are not to be missed. The **National Gallery of Canada**★★ *(380 Sussex Dr. 613-990-1985. Closed Mon.-Tues. late Sept.–early May)* is a glassy echo of the parliament buildings, its new home designed by Canadian-educated Moshe Safdie in 1988. Its strongest works are the 20th-century Canadian painters called the Group of Seven (see sidebar p. 87).

Similarly new and architecturally unique, Douglas Cardinal's curvaceous, copper-domed 1989 structure houses the **Canadian Museum of Civilization**★★ *(100 Laurier Ave. 819-776-7000. Closed Mon. mid-Oct.–April; adm. fee),* just across the Ottawa River in Hull, Quebec. Concentrating on Canadian history, aboriginal cultures, folk art, and archaeology, it has a popular children's museum and an IMAX/OMNIMAX film theater. The exhibits, which mix genuine artifacts with reproductions, have been as controversial as the architecture, but there's much that's worthwhile here, notably the hauntingly impressive totem poles in the Grand Hall.

National Gallery of Canada, Ottawa

Its name, nondescript building, and location some 20 minutes southeast of downtown may not be inspiring, but the **National Museum of Science and Technology**★ *(1867 St. Laurent Blvd. 613-991-3044. Closed Mon. Labor Day–April; adm. fee)* is one of Ottawa's most popular stops,

Canadian Museum of Civilization in Hull, with Parliament Hill across the river

where the hands-on Physics Hall is a perennial draw. Visitors to the **Canadian War Museum★** *(330 Sussex Dr. 819-776-8600. Closed Mon. mid-Oct.–April; adm. fee)* can see the re-creation of a World War One trench as part of the country's largest military history collection.

Quebec is a walkable bridge away from Ottawa, just over the Ottawa River. Aside from the Museum of Civilization, the most attractive destination in this area is **Gatineau Park★** *(Chelsea. 819-827-2020),* 140 square miles of hiking, skiing, fishing, and camping opportunities. Also in the park is **Kingsmere** *(Capitol Info. Centre 800-465-1867. Daily mid-June–mid-Oct., Wed.-Sun. mid-May–mid-June, grounds open year-round; adm. fee),* the country retreat of Canada's longest-serving prime minister, the eccentric William Lyon Mackenzie King, used until his death in 1950. It includes cottages, a museum and tearoom, and King's collection of architectural ruins.

Southwest of Ottawa on Hwy. 44 lies Lanark County, Canadian Shield country where farming yielded more stones than crops. Early Scottish and Irish settlers turned to textiles, most successfully in the case of ❷ **Almonte.** Ontario's own Mississippi River drops 62.5 feet here, and the resulting power made the village the Little Manchester of Canada, boasting more than eight woolen mills in the 1880s. One, the Rosamond Woolen Mill, now houses the **Mississippi Valley Textile Museum** *(3 Rosamond St. E. 613-256-3754. Mid-May–mid-Oct. Wed.-Sun., by appt. rest of year; adm. fee).*

North on Hwy. 15 is the **Mill of Kintail** *(RR 1. 613-256-3610. Mid-May–mid-Oct., by appt. rest of year; adm. fee),* Robert Tait McKenzie's romantic conversion of an 1830 gristmill into a summer home and studio. A medical pioneer in

Canadian Shield

The roadside from Ottawa to Kingston (and from Kingston to Morrisburg) is punctuated by the blockish, often rosy-colored stone that signals the southernmost part of the great Canadian Shield. Itself part of the Precambrian Shield, a crust of rocks nearly 4 billion years old, the Canadian Shield extends over 1.5 million sq. mi. from the Labrador Sea to the Arctic Ocean in a horseshoe shape to the St. Lawrence River (see map p. 6-7). In this part of Ontario, the rock is mostly hard granites and gneisses. Beloved of painters, cursed by farmers and railway builders, the Shield remains crucial to the Canadian psyche.

physical education, McKenzie (1867-1938) was also an artist, best known for his statues of athletes, some displayed here. The mill is the centerpiece of the **Mill of Kintail Conservation Area,** generously veined with hiking and ski trails.

South of Almonte on Trans-Canada 7, ❸ **Perth★** is an unexpectedly polished charmer in this rather hardscrabble region, an 1816 military settlement populated mainly by Lowland Scots and disbanded soldiers from the War of 1812. A self-guided walking tour brochure of Perth's elegant stone buildings is available at the old fire hall *(30 Herriott St. 613-267-3200)*; an 1840 house now contains the **Perth Museum** *(11 Gore St. E. 613-267-1947. Adm. fee).*

❹ **Kingston★★** *(Visitor Center, 209 Ontario St. 613-548-4415. Walking tour map available),* capital of the United Province of Canada in the 1840s, a port where Lake Ontario and the Rideau Canal flow into the St. Lawrence River, and home to Queen's University, it also possesses quiet 19th-century streets lined with prim limestone buildings. Stop at **Bellevue House★** *(35 Centre St. 613-545-8666. April-Oct., by appt. rest of year; adm. fee),* an Italianate villa and garden restored to the 1840s when John A. Macdonald, Canada's first prime minister, lived here.

Now finely restored, with a museum of military gear, a Children's Military Muster, and, in summer, daily drills, **Fort Henry★** *(Jct. of Hwys. 2 and 15. 613-542-7388. Late May–Sept.; adm. fee)* was upper Canada's most important stronghold in the 1860s. Then check out the legholds, files, and other grisly but fascinating objects on display at **The Correctional Service of Canada Museum** *(555 King St. W. 613-530-3122. Late May–Labor Day Wed.-Sun.),* located in the warden's residence near the historic Kingston Penitentiary, itself a monumental limestone deterrent to crime.

At Fort Henry, Kingston

Centrally situated in the Thousand Islands region, **Gananoque** began as a Loyalist settlement in 1789; today it's a summer resort, the big draw being a **boat cruise★** *(Gananoque Boat Line 613-382-2144. May–mid-Oct.; fare)* through the islands; the three-hour version includes a stop at Boldt Castle, begun in 1904 by the owner of New York's Waldorf-Astoria Hotel.

The Thousand Islands Parkway from Gananoque to Brockville is a relatively untrafficked stretch, marked by the squared-off pinkish outcroppings of the Canadian Shield (see sidebar p. 82). About 15 miles (24 km) from Gananoque, watch for Mallorytown Landing, mainland headquarters of **St. Lawrence Islands National Park** *(2 County Rd. 5. 613-923-5261. Adm. fee),* where a beach, walking trail, and interpretive exhibits on Canada's smallest national park spread over 21 islands or parts thereof.

❺ **Brockville,** an attractive Loyalist town, rises up from the St. Lawrence River in stately tiers. Architecture buffs may buy a self-guided walking tour map of Brockville's "best street," King Street East, from the Chamber of Commerce *(Blockhouse Island. 613-342-6553).*

St. Lawrence River and Thousand Islands

Just west of Prescott is **Fort Wellington National Historic Site★** *(613-925-2896. Mid-May–Sept., by appt. rest of year; adm. fee),* one of the best preserved and most appealing of Canada's forts. It figured in Canada-U.S. skirmishes in both 1813 and 1838. Many of the elite British rifle regiment stationed here kept their families in the blockhouse, giving the fort an unusually domestic character.

East of Morrisburg on Hwy. 2 is one of Ontario's finest destinations, ❻ **Upper Canada Village★★** *(Chrysler Park. 613-543-3704 or 800-437-2233. Mid-May–mid-Oct., call for off-season hours; adm. fee).* A composite re-creation of a pre-1867 St. Lawrence River village, it came into being in the 1950s when seven villages were flooded to make way for the St. Lawrence Seaway and some 30 structures were moved here. Plan to spend several hours watching costumed "inhabitants" explain the workings of their houses, printing presses, sawmill, farms, schools, and more.

Head north on Hwy. 31, then west on Hwy. 43 to delightful ❼ **Merrickville★,** an important settlement on the Rideau Canal, where the formidable **Blockhouse** *(Mill and Main Sts. Late May–mid-Oct.; adm. fee)* has become a local museum. Backtrack to Hwy. 16, and, before returning to Ottawa, go north to Manotick and **Watson's Mill** *(Mill St. 613-692-3571. June-Aug., by appt. rest of year; adm. fee).* Powered by the Rideau River since 1860, the five-story building houses a museum where you can master such arcana as cockle separators and smutters, plus watch the mill in action.

Toronto-London Loop★★

● 530 miles/850 km ● 3 to 5 days ● Spring, summer, and autumn are best but winter is very tolerable.

This extremely varied tour takes you through some of Canada's superlatives—beginning with Toronto, its biggest, richest, most artistically vibrant city, and passing through the prosperous farmland of southwestern Ontario, including the Mennonite areas in Waterloo County and the wine-growing region around Niagara. Along the way, there are two Great Lakes (Ontario and Erie) as well as enough smaller geographical, historical, and cultural diversions to suit the whole family.

Some of ❶ **Toronto**'s★★ *(Tourism Toronto 416-203-2600 or 800-362-1990)* sharpest visitors have made it sound admirable but bland—"New York run by the Swiss," according to Peter Ustinov, or "the city that works," in the words of Jane Jacobs. Be forewarned: Toronto's efficiency can make it seem deceptively easy to see and do all that the city offers.

One Toronto attraction appeals to everybody but real museum-phobes—the vast and venerable **Royal Ontario Museum**★★ *(100 Queen's Park. 416-586-8000. Adm. fee).* Whether your taste is for dinosaurs, bat caves, Chinese antiquities, European period rooms, Canadiana, or the spoils of ancient Egypt, it's all here.

CN Tower and Skydome, Toronto

Bay Street leading to the Financial District, Toronto

Art lovers will repair to the **Art Gallery of Ontario★★** *(317 Dundas St. W. 416-979-6648. Mid-May–mid-Oct. Tues.-Sun., Wed.-Sun. rest of year; adm. fee)* for its Inuit sculptures and European, American, and Canadian masterworks, and **The Grange,** the 19th-century Georgian house on the grounds. Then visit three outstanding boutique museums: the **George R. Gardiner Museum of Ceramic Art★** *(111 Queen's Park. 416-586-8080. Adm. fee includes Royal Ontario Museum);* the **Museum for Textiles★** *(55 Centre Ave. 416-599-5321. Closed Mon.; adm. fee);* and the newest of Toronto's museums, the **Bata Shoe Museum★** *(327 Bloor St. W. 416-979-7799. Closed Mon.; adm. fee).*

Toronto's premier historical attraction, **Fort York★** *(100 Garrison Rd. 416-392-6907. Adm. fee)* is the city's 1793 birthplace and the location of the Battle of York in 1813; in summer costumed staff demonstrate the various arts and crafts necessary for military life circa 1812.

The **Hockey Hall of Fame** *(Yonge St. at Front St. 416-360-7765. Adm. fee)* is home of the Stanley Cup and showcases the world's largest collection of hockey artifacts (housed in BCE Place, a smashing work of glass and steel incorporating old structures, worth seeing for itself).

Toronto's ethnic neighborhoods, full of Old World color, are one of the city's most appealing aspects: **Kensington Market** *(Kensington St. area, W of Spadina Ave.),* the old Jewish area; **Chinatown** *(Dundas St. and Spadina Ave.);* **The Danforth** *(Danforth Ave.),* the Greek neighborhood; **Corso Italia** *(St. Clair Ave. W. between Lansdowne Rd. and Dufferin St.),* and **Little Italy** *(College St. W. at Bathurst St.),* the original Italian area. **Black Creek Pioneer Village** *(Jane St. and Steeles Ave. W. 416-736-1733. May-Dec.; adm. fee)* is an 1860s pioneer village of over 35 buildings with a costumed staff. More commercial is **Paramount Canada's Wonderland**

(5 mi/8km E of Hwy. 400, Maple. 905-832-7000. Daily mid-May–Labor Day, weekends early May and Sept.–mid-Oct.; adm. fee), a 300-acre theme park with over 60 rides and attractions; a sea lion show; and a water park featuring slides, a wave pool, an interactive water jungle gym, and a river.

❷ **Kleinburg** is a bucolic village northwest of Toronto with an important art gallery, the **McMichael Canadian Art Collection**★★ *(Islington Ave. 905-893-1121. Closed Mon. mid-May–Oct.; adm. fee).* The Group of Seven (see sidebar this page) and their contemporary Tom Thomson, members of Canada's early modern school of primarily landscape painters, are the stars of the fine collection, which also showcases Inuit and First Nations works.

The **Ontario Agricultural Museum**★ in Milton *(off Hwy. 401. 905-878-8151. Call for hours; adm. fee)* hosts a notable collection of historic farm buildings, with wagon transportation around the big site. Except for this unusual museum, it's best to drive straight through Toronto's distended suburbs and satellite towns on Hwy. 401 to the Waterloo region and the busy, sprawling cities of **Kitchener–Waterloo** *(Visitor Center 519-748-0800),* which have several interesting museums. Among them: **Joseph Schneider Haus** *(466 Queen St. S. 519-742-7752. July-Aug., call for off-season hours; adm. fee)* , a Mennonite house restored to the 1850s, and **Woodside National Historic Site** *(528 Wellington St. N. 519-571-5684. May–early Jan.; adm. fee),* childhood home of Canadian Prime Minister William Lyon Mackenzie King (1874-1950), restored to the 1890s.

Two noteworthy specialty museums are the **Seagram Museum** *(57 Erb St. W. 519-885-1857. Closed Mon. Jan.-April),* devoted to the science and lore of alcoholic beverages and housed in part of the 19th-century Seagram distillery barrel warehouse (the remaining three-fourths of the museum is a modern exhibition building by architect Barton Myers), and the **Canadian Clay & Glass Gallery** *(25 Caroline St. N. 519-746-1882. Wed.-Sun.; adm. fee),* specializing in contemporary ceramics, glass, and enamel. If you're interested in Mennonite ways and byways, detour on Hwy. 86 as far as the villages of **Heidelberg** and **St. Jacobs,** as well as **Elmira** (on Rte. 21), where the gravelled shoulders of the roads are built to accommodate the black buggies. (St. Jacobs is very touristy and shop-ridden, but the country roads are not.)

❸ **Stratford**★, located west on Hwy. 7/8, has become the home of a major international theater festival while

Group of Seven

A loose-to-tight band of kindred spirits, Canada's most famous group of painters were not always seven (the number mounted to nine) nor a completely homogenous group. But they hauled Canadian painting into the modern age, giving vivid expression to their compatriots' profound connection to the land. Their dramatic, decorative style was inspired by the symbolists, Scandinavian expressionists, and their own work as graphic artists. Calling themselves Canada's National School almost from their first exhibition in 1920, the group disbanded in 1933. Look for canvases by J. E. H. MacDonald, A. Y. Jackson, Lawren Harris, and Tom Thomson (who died in 1917 before the Group's founding).

remaining a down-to-earth market town. Here, the play is the thing. The **Stratford Festival**★★ *(519-273-1600 or 800-567-1600. May-Nov.; adm. fee),* which began in 1953, occupies three theaters; its offerings always include several Shakespeare plays, contemporary drama, and a musical.

Southwest, straddling the Thames River and Trout Creek is the picturesque limestone town of **St. Marys**★ *(Off Hwy. 7/19, on Rte. 28).* Cottages, mansions, and public buildings made of local stone abound in this unspoiled mid-19th-century town. Of the two defunct quarries, one is used for recreational purposes.

One of Canada's first cheese factories (circa 1840) was built near Ingersoll, and the legendary 7,300-pound Big Cheese, which toured Great Britain in 1866, was a local triumph. Both are commemorated at the **Cheese Factory Museum** *(Centennial Park, N of Hwy. 401. 519-485-5510. Daily July-Aug., weekends May-June and Sept., or by appt.; donation).*

Hwy. 2 west will take you to **London,** a pleasant city dating from the 1800s. **Eldon House** *(481 Ridout St. N. 519-672-4580. Closed Mon.; adm. fee)* is the city's oldest residence, and includes a Victorian garden and art gallery. **Fanshawe Pioneer Village** *(Fanshawe Conservation Area, off Fanshawe Park Rd. 519-457-1296. May-Oct., call for off-season hours; adm. fee)* has 22 buildings dedicated to Ontario's rural beginnings, while the ❹ **Ska-Nah-Doht Iroquoian Village** *(Longwoods Rd. Conservation Area, Hwy. 2 W of Hwy. 402. 519-264-2420. Closed Sat.-Sun. Labor Day–late May; adm. fee)* recreates a local Iroquoian village of a thousand years ago.

Entering **St. Thomas** *(Visitor Center, 555 Talbot St. 519-631-1981. Walking tour pamphlet available)* on Hwy. 3, look to the right for the jovial larger-than-life statue of Jumbo, a Barnum

Paddlers on the Avon River, Stratford

& Bailey celebrity elephant killed here by a Grand Trunk Railway locomotive in 1885. Down the street, period rooms at the **Elgin County Pioneer Museum** *(32 Talbot St. 519-631-6537. Closed Mon.; adm. fee)* focus on social and economic history. This area, surrounding the circa 1822 Gothic Revival **Old St. Thomas Church** *(55 Walnut St. Late May–Labor Day),* is one of the oldest and most interesting parts of town.

Cheese Factory Museum barn, Ingersoll

To the east, little **Aylmer** *(Visitor Center 519-773-9723)* affords extraordinary views of tundra swans migrating by the thousands from the end of February through the start of April. Turn north onto Hwy. 73 (John St.) from Hwy. 3 (Talbot St.), and follow signs for the Ontario Police College, which is next to the **Aylmer Wildlife Management Area★.** An elevated viewing stand looks out over a marshy world of flooded fields and artificial ponds, patronized by ducks and other wildfowl even when the tundra swans are absent.

Rejoin Hwy. 3 heading east. At Courtland, take Hwy. 59 south to **Backus Heritage Conservation Area** *(Off Hwy. 59. 519-586-2201. May-Oct., by appt. rest of year; adm. fee)* in Port Rowan, an ensemble of some 15 pioneer buildings. Visit the nature center or walk the Carolinian trails in the **Backus Woods.** Continue south as far as you can go, to ❺ **Long Point Provincial Park★★** *(519-586-2133),* the Great Lakes' wildest and most varied sandspit. A biosphere reserve recognized by UNESCO, Long Point is 20 miles long and thought to be 4,000 years old. It's a staging area for migratory songbirds and waterfowl, and populated by birds, turtles, fish, reptiles, and amphibians.

Follow Rte. 42, Hwy. 24, and Hwy. 6 east toward Port Dover. Though Lake Erie is close by, it is frustratingly hidden from view for a considerable stretch by **Turkey Point Provincial Park** *(519-426-3239).* It's clearly visible at **Port Dover,** the classic lake port, thronged in summer by tourists walking the boardwalk, fishing in what's called the world's largest freshwater fishing port, or feasting on Lake Erie perch.

Take Hwy. 6 north and Rte. 3 east, past tobacco farms and rustic villages, to **Port Colborne,** the southernmost point on the Welland Canal. The **Port Colborne Historical**

and Marine Museum *(280 King St. 905-834-7604. May-Dec.)* highlights the town's connection to the canal.

Among **Fort Erie**'s numerous attractions are two stellar sites. **Historic Fort Erie★** *(Niagara Pkwy. and Lakeshore Dr. 905-871-0540. Mid-May–Sept.; adm. fee),* a much beleaguered fort, was established in 1764, destroyed by the Americans in 1813, and now restored as a living history site. If your interests tend to the domestic, repair to Bertie Hall, an 1835 building that houses the **Mildred M. Mahoney Silver Jubilee Dolls' House Gallery★** *(657 Niagara Blvd. 905-871-5833. May-Dec., by appt. rest of year; adm. fee),* a cornucopia of more than 200 dollhouses dating from 1780 to the present.

There's one must-do in ❻ **Niagara Falls★★** *(N on Queen Elizabeth Way. Visitor Center 905-356-6061 or 800-563-2557),* and that's obvious, free, and equally spectacular in all four seasons: the **falls★★** themselves. A trip on a ***Maid of the Mist***★★ *(5920 River Rd. 905-358-5781. May–late Oct.; fare),* one of four sturdy boats that have been ferrying visitors around the falls for 150 years, is highly recommended. Or try the **Niagara Spanish Aero Car** *(Niagara Pkwy., 3 mi/4.8 km N of falls. 905-356-2241. March-Nov.; fare);* the suspended cable car crosses a giant whirlpool, formed at the end of the rapids downstream from the falls. The town of Niagara Falls itself has been considerably spruced up lately, but still has plenty of souvenir stalls. For fans of Granny's attic, the **Niagara Falls Museum** *(5651 River Rd. 905-356-2151. Adm. fee)* is a charmer, with 700,000-plus artifacts.

Niagara Falls from *Maid of the Mist*

Niagara-on-the-Lake★★ *(Visitor Center 905-468-4263),* located northeast on Hwy. 55, is Ontario's other theater town. Unlike Stratford, this historic town has a radiance emanating from its immaculate buildings constructed after the War of 1812. Capital of upper Canada in the 1790s, burned by the Americans in 1813, a summer resort at the turn of the century—Niagara-on-the-Lake has had several incarnations,

Royal Botanical Gardens, Hamilton

most recently as home of the **Shaw Festival★★** *(905-468-2172 or 800-511-7429. April-Oct.)*, devoted to work written by George Bernard Shaw and his contemporaries and home to one of the finest acting ensembles in North America. **Fort George National Historic Site★★** *(Off Niagara Pkwy. 905-468-4257. Daily April-Oct., grounds open Mon.-Fri. and by appt. rest of year; adm. fee)*, a restoration of the fort built by the British in 1796 to replace Fort Niagara, is an excellent introduction to the region's military history.

Take the Queen Elizabeth Way to **Hamilton,** a steel-manufacturing city, where the **Art Gallery of Hamilton★** *(123 King St. W. 905-527-6610. Wed.-Sun.; adm. fee)* has one of Canada's best collections of North American and European art. **Dundurn Castle** *(York Blvd., Dundurn Park. 905-546-2872. Closed Mon.; adm. fee)*, a 40-plus-room Italianate villa, is restored to its mid-19th-century heyday. Take time to visit the **Royal Botanical Gardens★★** *(Plains Rd. at Hwys. 403 and 6. 905-527-1158. Adm. fee)*, one of the seven wonders of Ontario—2,700 acres that include an acre of irises, two acres of roses, the world's largest lilac collection, and a wildlife sanctuary.

Off Hwy. 2 in **Burlington,** the 1800 **Joseph Brant Museum** *(1240 North Shore Blvd. E. 905-634-3556. Closed Mon., Sat. by appt.; adm. fee)* commemorates the charismatic Mohawk leader and Loyalist, Joseph Brant (ca 1742-1807) in his last house.

The prosperous Toronto suburb of **Oakville** offers a look into its past at the **Oakville Museum** *(905-845-3541. Closed Mon.; adm. fee)*, which includes the 1856 Customs House; **Erchless** *(8 Navy St.)*, an estate restored to 1925; and the 1835 **Old Post Office** *(Lakeside Park)*.

Niagara Wineries

What do Burgundy, Champagne, parts of Germany, and the Niagara Peninsula have in common? A cool-climate growing season amenable to grape production. The Niagara Peninsula has an added benefit—the protective embrace of Lakes Erie and Ontario and the Niagara Escarpment, which makes for a mild microclimate. Almost 200 years ago, about the time the first grapes were planted here, a visitor noted the region's temperate winters and the "exuberance of the soil." Four out of every five wine grapes grown in Canada come from the Niagara region, with whites, and particularly a dessert wine called icewine, enjoying remarkable success. Look for road signs that say Wine Route: More than 20 wineries, stretching roughly from Niagara Falls to Winona, offer tours and tastings. *(Wine Council of Canada 905-684-8070 or 888-794-6379)*

Winnipeg Circle

● 200 miles/325 km ● 2 to 3 days ● May to October

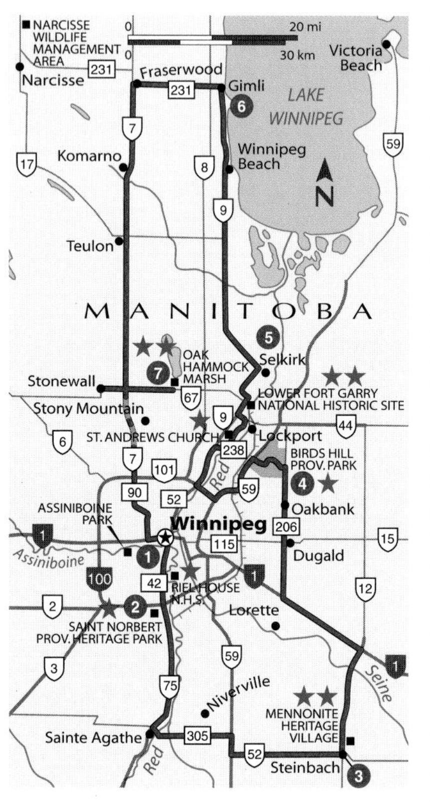

This rich, varied, and relatively short jaunt begins in Winnipeg and takes a quick lap around southeastern Manitoba's prairies. The trip has its scenic moments, but focuses more on the region's museums, historic places, and ethnic traditions. Sites around Winnipeg run the gambit from geology exhibits to fighter planes to bronze nudes, but several pay close attention to the heritages of First Nations peoples, the Métis, and French-Canadians. There's a stop to learn about the Mennonite tradition, and there are several vivid reminders of the 19th-century English. The route pauses at the shore of Lake Winnipeg before looping back.

One of the oldest settlements in western Canada, ❶ **Winnipeg** *(Tourism Winnipeg 204-943-1970 or 800-665-0204)* lies along an ancient travel route at the confluence of the Red and Assiniboine Rivers. Site of several fur-trading posts beginning in the 1730s, then an agricultural colony, railroad town, and now a major commercial center, Winnipeg boasts a splendid mix of ethnic heritage, many fine historic buildings, an extensive park system, and excellent museums of art, nature, and history.

Begin downtown at **The Forks National Historic Site**★ *(E of Main St. 204-983-6757)*, a riverside park with dozens of shops, restaurants, and market stalls crowded among several restored railroad buildings. Rent a canoe and drift along this historic stretch of water, or stroll around the bend and tour the **Manitoba Legislative Building** *(450 Broadway Ave., between Osborne and Kennedy Sts. 204-945-5813. Building open daily, tours July–Labor Day Mon.-Fri.)*, a mammoth 1920 neoclassic beauty. Also within the park, turn the kids loose at the **Manitoba Children's Museum**★★ *(45 Forks Market Rd. 204-956-1888. Adm. fee)*, where hands-on exhibits allow them to interview Mom on

TV, morph Dad's face on a computer, climb around in a vintage locomotive, and learn about animals.

Next, cross the river into Winnipeg's French Quarter, Saint Boniface, western Canada's largest French-speaking community. At the heart of the neighborhood stands the imposing stone shell of **Saint Boniface Basilica★,** which burned in 1968. It overlooks an old cemetery where you'll find the grave of Louis Riel, leader of the Red River Resistance of 1869, founder of Manitoba, and martyr to Métis independence (see sidebar p. 95). Just across the lawns, visit the **Saint Boniface Museum★** *(204-237-4500. Daily May-Sept., Mon.-Fri. Oct.-April; adm. fee),* housed in a huge oak-log building. Constructed in 1846 as a hospital and convent, it tracks the area's history from the voyageurs forward.

Saint Boniface, Winnipeg's French Quarter

Back on the west bank, explore Winnipeg's **Exchange District★** *(Begins at Portage and Main Sts.),* several blocks of old banks, hotels, and warehouses representing various architectural styles from the 1880s to the 1920s. Then drop by the **Manitoba Museum of Man and Nature★★** *(190 Rupert Ave. at Main St. 204-956-2830. Closed Mon. Labor Day–mid-May; adm. fee)* and knock around the decks and cabins of the ***Nonsuch*★★,** a magnificent, full-size replica of the ketch that sailed from England to Hudson Bay in 1668 and led to the founding of the Hudson's Bay Company. Other exhibits illustrate Manitoba's major habitat zones, First Nations cultures, and early Winnipeg. Here, too, are a planetarium and a hands-on science gallery.

Also downtown, visit the **Crafts Museum** *(183 Kennedy St. 204-943-1190. Mon.-Sat.; donation)* for its native and European handiwork; the **Winnipeg Art Gallery★** *(300 Memorial Blvd. 204-786-6641. Closed Mon. Labor Day–mid-June; adm. fee)* for its wonderful collection of contemporary Inuit art; and the **Dalnavert Museum★** *(61 Carlton St. 204-943-2835. Sat.-Sun. Jan.-Feb., closed Mon. and Fri. March-Dec.; adm. fee),* a painstakingly restored 1895 Queen Anne house.

For a whiff of grass, a pool of shade, and the gurgle of running water, drive west on Corydon Ave. to **Assini-**

Manitoba farm off Hwy. 7 near Winnipeg

boine Park. Here you'll find the **Leo Mol Sculpture Garden★★** *(204-237-1622. Closed Mon. late May–late Sept.),* where the celebrated Ukrainian artist's bronzes of polar bears, religious figures, and nudes stand amid a formal landscape of walkways and shrubs. Visit Mol's studio and learn how he cast his statues. An English garden adjoins the sculpture area, and howls from across the road guide you to the **Assiniboine Park Zoo** *(204-986-6921. Adm. fee).*

Near the airport, visit the **Western Canada Aviation Museum★** *(958 Ferry Ave. near W end of Ellice Ave., poorly marked. 204-786-5503. Adm. fee),* a collection of beautifully restored World War II fighters, bush planes, and prop-driven passenger planes. Farther west, at the **Living Prairie Museum** *(2795 Ness Ave. 204-832-0167. Tours late April–June Sun., July-Aug. Sun.-Fri.),* ramble through a vest pocket remnant of the tallgrass prairie that once covered much of southern Manitoba. For a more detailed analysis of grasslands and wetlands, visit the **Fort Whyte Centre★** *(1961 McCreary Rd. 204-989-8355. Adm. fee),* where acres of marsh, small lakes, and prairie are made inviting by floating boardwalks, shaded paths, and benches tucked into corners likely for spotting wildlife. At the Visitor Center, look in on pens of ducklings or go nose to nose with a huge walleye.

On Winnipeg's southern outskirts, **Riel House National Historic Site★** *(330 River Rd. 204-257-1783. Mid-May–Labor Day)* preserves the small Red River frame house built in 1880 for Louis Riel's mother. The site recounts the family's tragic history, while celebrating the culture of the Métis—descendants of native peoples and European fur traders.

From Winnipeg, take Hwy. 75 south to ❷ **St. Norbert Provincial Heritage Park★** *(204-642-6076. June-Sept. Thurs.-Mon.)* and tour two restored houses. One, the home of a county clerk, reflects life in a French-speaking Métis settlement circa 1880. The second, a large and cleverly designed farmhouse, illustrates how a prosperous French-Canadian farm family lived at the turn of the century.

Continue south to Sainte Agathe, then jog east on Rte. 305 and Hwy. 52 to ❸ **Steinbach** and the **Mennonite Heritage Village★★** *(N of town on Hwy. 12. 204-326-9661. Most bldgs. open May-Sept., main gallery open year-round; adm. fee),* 40 acres with buildings ranging from a humble sod hut to spacious house-barns, shops, churches, and a large Dutch windmill. Track the Mennonite history of overcoming religious persecution, then step into the village, where blacksmiths tinker with steel and fellows in overalls fiddle with antique farm machinery and tend the farm animals. The Livery Barn Restaurant serves Mennonite fare.

On Rte. 206 head north over rolling farmland into ❹ **Birds Hill Provincial Park★** *(5 mi/8 km N of Oakbank. 204-222-9151. Adm. fee),* where prairie hills and woodlands surround a shallow artificial lake with a beach ideal for small children.

From the park's west gate, turn south on Hwy. 59, west on Hwy. 101, then north on Hwy. 9 to Rte. 238, also called the **River Road Heritage Parkway★.** This pleasant back road hugs the Red River and passes several buildings reflecting a strong 19th-century English presence,

Louis Riel

Born in 1844, Louis Riel headed up the 1869 Red River Resistance, which led to Manitoba's entry into the Confederation where the traditional land ownership patterns and French language of the Métis people were recognized. Forced into exile for his role, Riel later went to Saskatchewan to lead the Métis in a similar struggle during the North West Rebellion of 1885. He was tried, convicted of treason, and hanged in Regina on Nov. 16, 1885.

St. Andrews Rectory National Historic Site

including **St. Andrews Church★** *(S of Lockport),* a relatively small fieldstone edifice, completed in 1849 and furnished with simple pews and buffalo-hide kneelers. Loiter in the graveyard among headstones dating from the 1840s, then cross the lane to **St. Andrews Rectory National Historic Site★** *(204-334-6405. Mid-May–early Sept.; donation),* which traces Anglican missionary activities in an 1854 house. Just up the road, stir a cup of tea at the **Captain Kennedy Museum and Tea House★** *(River Road. 204-338-5105. May-Sept.; donation),* rustic, gracious, and built of stone in 1866 by William Kennedy, trader, magistrate, and explorer.

Marine Museum of Manitoba, Selkirk

Most of the English along the Red River prospered under the immense Hudson's Bay Company trading post just downstream at **Lower Fort Garry National Historic Site★★** *(Hwy. 9. 204-785-6050. Mid-May–early Sept.; adm. fee).* Begun in 1830 and enclosed by a high wall, this compound is the oldest intact stone fur-trading post in North America. Restored, stocked, and staffed to resemble the 1850s, it offers an exceptionally detailed portrait of the fur trade.

Farther north in ❺ **Selkirk,** climb aboard an 1897 steamship at the **Marine Museum of Manitoba★** *(Selkirk Park, Queen and Eveline Sts. 204-482-7761. Daily May-Aug., Sat.-Sun. Sept.; adm. fee),* which preserves six large vessels that plied Lake Winnipeg and other inland waters. Beached but restored, the ships are stuffed with marine artifacts.

Fold out your beach chair at ❻ **Gimli,** once an Icelandic fishing village and now a resort town on the southwestern shore of Lake Winnipeg. Then take Rte. 231 west and Hwy. 7 south to **Stonewall,** where the ruins of three lime kiln towers overlook a pleasant beach at **Stonewall Quarry Park** *(204-467-5354. Call for hours; fee for swimming).*

Wrap up your tour at the ❼ **Oak Hammock Marsh Interpretive Centre★★** *(Hwy. 67. 204-467-3300. Adm. fee),* with a guided canoe outing among the cattails and backwaters of a reclaimed marsh teeming with birds, mammals, reptiles, and amphibians. A floating boardwalk and bird blind, an indoor observation area, computer programs, hands-on exhibits—all this and more offer a fascinating glimpse of a woefully underrated ecosystem.

Garter Snakes

Every spring, from late April to mid-May, tens of thousands of red-sided garter snakes tangle in slithering, Medusa-like mating balls at the **Narcisse Wildlife Management Area** *(204-745-6799).* To reach the herpetological passion pits, go north on Hwy. 17 from Teulon and drive 4 miles (6.5 km) beyond Narcisse. Along the way, gawk at the statue of two giant snakes, Sam and Sarah, at Inwood.

Parks and Prairies

● 600 miles/970 km ● 2 to 3 days ● May to October

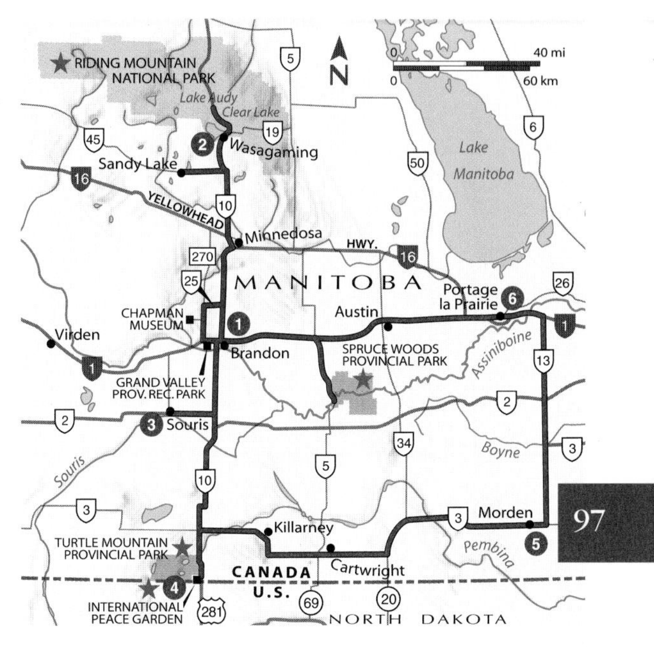

This bucolic ramble among the rolling prairie hills, highlands, and river valleys of western Manitoba loops through the heart of the region's richest farm country. Museums here tend to emphasize turn-of-the-century rural life, with a special reverence for the grand steam-powered tractors and other complex farm gadgetry that signaled the arrival of the industrial age. But there are some surprises, such as a Cretaceous marine reptile museum and the International Peace Park, marking Canada's border with the United States with a swath of flowers.

The route starts in ❶ **Brandon** *(Visitor Center 204-728-3287 or 888-799-1111),* a once booming 1880s railroad hub, now a major agricultural center and university town along the Assiniboine River. Trains and grain built the city's attractive downtown area, but airplanes and fighter pilots kept

Clear Lake, Riding Mountain National Park

Brandon jumping during World War II. For a glimpse of how crews prepared for combat, drop by the **Commonwealth Air Training Plan Museum★** *(At the airport. 204-727-2444. Adm. fee),* which displays restored vintage aircraft as well as bomb sights, machine guns, radar scopes, radios, parachutes, staff cars, and an extensive archive.

Souris Swinging Bridge

West of Brandon, visit **The Stott Site** *(Grand Valley Provincial Recreation Park. 204-726-6441),* a bison-kill site where prehistoric hunters drove the beasts into an enclosure made of brush (now reconstructed).

North of Brandon, and a bit hard to find, the **Chapman Museum** *(5 mi/8 km N on Rte. 270, then W 5 mi/8 km on gravel road. 204-728-7396. Donation)* recalls the region's pioneer days in 16 old-timey buildings stacked to the rafters with cream separators, kitchen gadgets, tools, toys, and other neat stuff.

Follow Hwy. 10 north over a boundless prairie landscape that eventually tilts up toward the highlands of **Riding Mountain National Park★** *(204-848-7275. Adm. fee).* Part of the Manitoba escarpment, this varied and rambling preserve offers loads of trails, beaches, and a chance to see large black bears, bison, moose, elk, deer, and wolves. Get your bearings at the park's Visitor Center *(204-848-7249. Mid-May–Sept.)* in the woodsy resort hamlet of ❷ **Wasagaming** on the south shore of spring-fed **Clear Lake.** For a quick overview of the park's geology, climate, and vegetation, follow Hwy. 10 around the lake and north to the short **Boreal Island loop trail.** Farther north, climb **Agassiz Tower** and gaze across the plains. Returning south, take Lake Audy Road to the **Bison Enclosure,** where roughly two dozen plains bison graze, ruminate, and roll in the wildflowers. At **Lake Katherine** *(Just E of Clear Lake),* enjoy the drums, dancing, and traditional native foods offered by Anishinabe Camp and Cultural Tours *(off Hwy. 19. 204-848-2815. May-Sept.; adm. fee).*

South of Riding Mountain N.P., Hwy. 45 leads west to **Sandy Lake,** a small farm town with two lovely Ukrainian churches: one Orthodox, one Catholic, each capped by silver onion domes and lavishly decorated inside.

Buffalo ... or Bison?

Misled by the likes of buffalo chips and Buffalo Bill, many believe that the western portion of North America was once populated by magnificent herds of buffalo. Not so. These shaggy creatures are really bison; it is their African and Asian cousins that are properly termed buffalo. Driven to the brink of extinction around the turn of the century, the bison population has recovered strongly. Seeing a bison is now quite common; but seeing a buffalo? Now that would be the stuff of legend.

Retrace the drive south on Hwy. 10 through Brandon and detour west to the old railroad and farming community of ❸ **Souris.** Poke around the **Hillcrest Museum** *(26 Crescent Ave. E. 204-483-2008. Daily July-Aug., Sun. mid-May–June and Sept.; adm. fee),* a creaking 1910 mansion stuffed with antiques, memorabilia, and odd items such as a treadle-driven dentist drill. The nearby 582-foot **Souris Swinging Bridge,** Canada's longest simple, single-span suspension bridge, bestrides the Souris River with planks just wide enough for two adults to stroll along hand in hand.

Farther south along Hwy. 10, kick back at **Turtle Mountain Provincial Park**★ *(204-534-7204. Adm. fee),* a wooded highland of gently rolling hills. Dotted with more than 200 small lakes, this oasis of shaded footpaths, bike trails, and beaches offers a welcome break from the prairies and a chance to see moose, white-tailed deer, and loons.

Just south, stroll among regimented beds of pansies, peonies and daffodils at the ❹ **International Peace Garden**★ *(204-534-2510. Adm. fee during peak bloom mid-May–mid-Sept.),* which straddles the border between Canada and the United States and celebrates generations of friendship between the nations. Every year gardeners plant roughly 120,000 annuals along an extensive promenade of brick walkways, low walls, fountains, ponds, towers, and reflecting pools.

International Peace Garden

Next, backtrack to Hwy. 3 and drive east through the Pembina River Valley. This course skirts the route taken by the International Boundary Commission in 1872-73, and by the North West Mounted Police as they headed for Alberta in 1874. In **Cartwright,** drop by the **Blacksmith Shop Museum**★ *(Bowles and N. Railway Sts. 204-529-2486. June-Aug.)* and imagine earning your keep on the lineshaft, a menacing contraption composed of large pulleys and great flapping belts that power a drill press, trip-hammer, and grinding wheels.

Continue east to ❺ **Morden** *(Chamber of Commerce 204-822-5630),* an 1880s railroad town with architecture of the period. Amble through the shaded lanes and extensive plantings of the **Agriculture and Agri-Food Canada Research Centre** *(1st and Stephen Sts. 204-822-4471. May-Sept.)*. Then head for the **Morden and District Museum★** *(Recreation Centre, 2nd and Gilmour Sts. 204-822-3406. June-Aug. afternoons; adm. fee)* to gape at the startling eye socket in the mosasaur skull and 40-foot spine of the huge marine lizard that swam nearby during the Cretaceous period. The museum also displays Cretaceous fossils of fish, a turtle, a large flattened squid, various pelvises, flippers, and teeth.

East of Morden, the **Pembina Threshermen's Museum★** *(Hwy. 3. 204-325-7497. May-Oct. Sat.-Thurs.; adm. fee)* lovingly maintains a large collection of steam-powered farm machinery—tractors, threshers, feed cutters, crushers—as well as early gas-powered tractors, miniature steam locomotives, and a vast array of implements for barn and household. The grounds also include a few old houses, a lovely 1903 train depot, a sawmill, and a church.

Blacksmith Shop Museum, Cartwright

Head north to catch Trans-Canada 1 back to Brandon. Near ❻ **Portage la Prairie,** the **Fort la Reine Museum and Pioneer Village** *(Jct. of Hwys. 1A and 26. 204-857-3259. Mid-May–mid-Sept.; adm. fee)* is worth a stop just to cringe at the Frankensteinian hair curler and the X-ray shoefitter (talk about progress!). West, near Austin, the **Manitoba Agricultural Museum** *(Hwy. 34S. 204-637-2354. Mid-May–Sept.; adm. fee)* shows off its large collection of operating vintage farm machinery as well as a Homesteader's Village depicting rural life in late 19th-century Manitoba.

Finally, head for **Spruce Woods Provincial Park★** *(Hwy. 5 12.5 mi/20 km S of Trans-Canada 1. 204-834-3223. Adm. fee),* an intimate landscape of woods, marsh, and open meadows full of long grass and willowy prairie wildflowers. Of particular interest are the **Spirit Sands★,** 1.5 square miles of open sand buffeted into dunes by the wind and slowly succumbing to the advance of grasses, shrubs, and trees. This tiny spot is part of a vast sand delta deposited by the Assiniboine River at the end of the last ice age. The rest of the delta, which covered 2,500 square miles, now lies under a rich layer of vegetation. Venture out into the sand on foot, or ride a horse-drawn wagon *(fee).*

Regina Ramble★

● **575 miles/925 km** ● **4 to 5 days** ● **May to October**

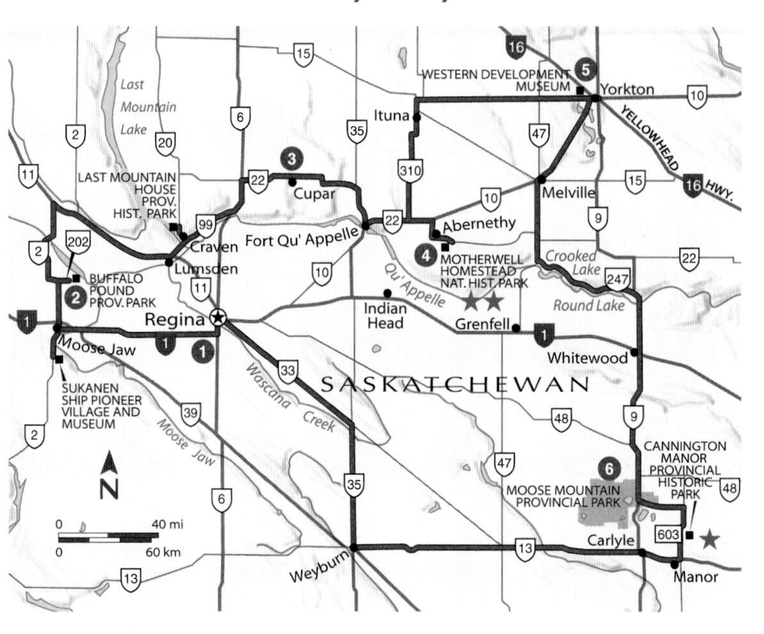

The land this drive traverses is mostly flat, but the past gives it shape and character. Historical museums dominate this tour, repeating the themes of First Nations, the fur trade, immigration, and settlement. And not everywhere is flat; rivers flow through sheltered valleys, and forest covers a gentle highland.

As the capital of Saskatchewan, tree-lined ❶ **Regina** *(Visitor Center 306-789-5099 or 800-661-5099)* represents a mighty transformation. Its early name, Pile O'Bones, referred to its siting at the treeless junction of a bison trail and a prairie creek, known for a mound of bison bones stacked up by native hunters. In little more than a century, so much has changed. Planners in the late 1800s and the early 1900s anticipated a provincial population many times Saskatchewan's current size, resulting in one of the world's largest urban complexes and one of

Government House, Regina

Regina's chief assets, **Wascana Centre★★.** Its primary structure, the **Saskatchewan Legislative Building★** *(306-787-5358. Tours daily)* also reflects grand aspirations, with 34 different types of marble, architecture borrowed from European palaces, and an assembly chamber filled with 58 of the originally projected 125 members.

Across the waters of Wascana Lake stands the **Royal Saskatchewan Museum★** *(2445 Albert St. 306-787-2815).* Start at the geology exhibit, and proceed through displays of prehistoric life. There's much to explore: Walk the bottom of a shallow sea while a mosasaur swims overhead, ogle the fantastically huge giant bison, or visit a Plains Indian winter camp and listen to stories of native life.

Next, match eyeballs with an 8.5-foot Burmese python named Stretch or take in the latest IMAX show at the **Saskatchewan Science Centre★** *(Winnipeg St. and Wascana Dr. 306-791-7914. Adm. fee).* Then see what's showing in the spacious rooms of the **MacKenzie Art Gallery★** *(3475 Albert St. 306-522-4242).*

Northwest of Wascana Centre, sample imperial elegance on a tour of **Government House★** *(4607 Dewdney Ave. 306-787-5717. Closed Mon.),* official residence of lieutenant governors from 1891 to 1945. It is now restored to the time of Lt. Governor Forget, who lived here at the turn of the century.

Royal Canadian Mounted Police recruits, "Depot" Division

Another great tradition awaits a short distance west at the **"Depot" Division,** home of the Royal Canadian Mounted Police Training Academy and the **RCMP Centennial Museum★** *(Dewdney Ave. W. 306-780-5838. Donation).* The story of the Mounties, since their beginnings in 1873, is essentially a history of western Canada. Soak in tales of frontier daring at the museum, then join a guided tour past marching cadets.

Leaving Regina, Trans-Canada 1 barrels through wheat fields, then drops into the shelter of a river bottom at **Moose Jaw** *(Visitor Center 306-693-8097).* Grab a map at 445 Main Street North and tour the historic district, paying attention to the murals on the old brick buildings. Or burrow beneath the streets in the **Tunnels of Little Chicago**

(108 Main St. N. 306-693-5261. Fee for tours), a network of secret passageways that once sheltered illegal immigrants and—during the Roaring Twenties—bootleggers and gangsters from across the U.S. border.

Admire vehicles of all kinds at the **Western Development Museum★★** *(50 Diefenbaker Dr. 306-693-5989. Closed Mon. Jan.-March; adm. fee).* From birch-bark canoes to jet aircraft, trains, cars, and some very odd contraptions, the museum celebrates the human urge to be carried around. Too bad you can't try out the velocipede, or giddyup on Blowtorch, the mechanical walking horse.

Moose monument, Moose Jaw

Oddest of all might be the vessel at **Sukanen Ship Pioneer Village and Museum★** *(8 mi/13 km S on Hwy. 2. 306-693-7315. June–mid-Sept.; adm. fee).* The large collection of historical buildings and artifacts includes the bizarre-looking hand-built craft of Tom Sukanen, who dreamed of sailing it home to Finland, but never got it near the water. His story is both tragic and inspiring.

Escape north on Hwy. 2 to the Qu'Appelle River Valley and ❷ **Buffalo Pound Provincial Park** *(306-693-2678. Adm. fee).* Scan the hills for bison, then grab binoculars and head into the **Nicolle Flats Interpretive Area★,** a rich marshland filled with birds. The floating boardwalk allows entry to the watery world of bitterns, rails, and water-tiger beetles lurking in 10-foot-high reed grass.

From here, stay on the high prairie to Craven via Lumsden, then head north on Hwy. 20 to **Last Mountain House Provincial Historic Park** *(306-787-2700. July-Aug. Fri.-Mon.),* a Hudson's Bay Company provisioning post from 1869 to 1871, its main mission to supply northern posts with pemmican—dried bison. The buildings may seem small, but think of them as the only ones for hundreds of miles, and they grow in stature.

Many Saskatchewan towns have community museums, some of distinctly local interest. You can see someone's mug collection, or stacks of old high school yearbooks. But many are worth visiting if only to hear locals talk about the items and tell stories triggered by them. Two such places are the ❸ **Cupar and District Heritage Museum** *(Cupar. 306-723-4324. Sun. and Wed.; donation);*

The Mounties

Established in 1873 to patrol the Canadian West, the North West Mounted Police—also called Red Coats, Riders of the Plains, and the Mounties—put a stop to the devastating American whiskey trade in Canada. In addition, the police established a Canadian presence beside the restless American frontier, and helped chart a peaceful course between settlers and natives. In 1920 the force received its current name, the Royal Canadian Mounted Police.

and the **Fort Qu'Appelle Museum** *(3rd St., Fort Qu'Appelle. 306-332-6443. June-Aug.; adm. fee),* on the grounds of a former Hudson's Bay Company post.

Follow Hwy. 22 past Abernethy and look for signs to ❹ **Motherwell Homestead National Historic Site**★★ *(306-333-2116. Mid-May–Sept., call for off-season hours; adm. fee).* Built in 1897, the fieldstone Italianate farmhouse is a surprising sight—until you learn the determination of William Motherwell, an Ontario immigrant and later Canada's minister of agriculture, "to reverse the idea that farming is a subservient occupation." By the looks of it, he succeeded. The farmstead has been restored to its 1912 condition. Backtrack to Hwy. 310, then head toward **Yorkton,** pausing beside any of the numerous **prairie potholes**—little nature reserves filled with muskrats, grebes, ducks, coots, and small wading birds that hide in the tall grass until you've sat quietly for long enough to be forgotten. Each of these is a delightful scene of summer's growth. Multiplied by over a million, these seemingly insignificant ponds attract the great migratory flocks of autumn and spring.

Yorkton's ❺ **Western Development Museum**★ *(Hwy. 16 W of town. 306-783-8361. May-Sept.; adm. fee)* focuses on the immigrants who settled Saskatchewan. Drawn by the promise of free land, and hoping for religious and cultural freedom, immigrants arrived in their national dress carrying whatever they could afford to bring. Most of us can find something of our own ancestors in their stories.

Railside grain elevators, Yorkton

Accentuating that diversity, the parish bulletin at **St. Mary's Ukrainian Catholic Church** *(155 Catherine St. 306-783-7778. Daily in summer, by appt. rest of year)* is still printed in both English and Ukrainian. Drop by to view the interior of the dome, painted to depict the heavenly coronation of Mary.

It is a short drive to Melville, where the **Melville Heritage Museum** *(306-728-2070. May-Oct. Tues.-Sun.; donation)* fills the former Luther Academy with displays related to its history as a school, orphanage, and nursing home.

St. Mary's Ukrainian church, Yorkton

From here, take Hwy. 47 to Hwy. 247 through what one resident called "the only thing that passes for scenery around here," the lovely Qu'Appelle River Valley. Keep an eye out for a kiosk on the slope just above the road, where an informational plaque tells of the **Moose Bay Burial Mound,** constructed 950 years ago by Plains Indians.

Down the road at Whitewood is the most eccentric and peculiar display of the arcane in the region. **Old George's Authentic Collectibles**★ *(306-735-2255. June-Aug.; fee for tours)* is the result of one man's lifetime passion for gathering things. George Chopping has crammed a prairie mansion with antique bottles, furniture, tools, native artifacts, toys, inkwells, marbles, fruit crates, Victrolas, and just about anything that's ever been bought or sold at a garage sale.

Ascend to the *un*dizzying but pleasant heights of ❻ **Moose Mountain Provincial Park** *(306-577-2131. Adm. fee in summer),* an elevated plateau covered with lakes, marshes, and mixed broadleaf forest. The core area is a lakeside resort, while the rest is wild, little traveled, and loaded with wildlife. Walk the Beaver Lake Nature Trail, or give in to the kids and hit the water slides.

An interesting footnote in Saskatchewan's history can be read at **Cannington Manor Provincial Historic Park**★ *(NE of Carlyle. 306-787-2700. Mid-May–Labor Day Wed.-Mon.; adm. fee).* Founded in the 1880s, the settlement attempted to establish a prairie version of British country life, with all its social conventions. Explore what remains of the village, learning the odd story of bachelor "remittance men," and perhaps shooting a couple wickets of croquet.

Turning back toward Regina, the drive's last leg cruises the flat, flat plains. Picture it 150 years ago: not a tree, the prairie never broken by a plow, occasional dark herds of bison. It's a strong image to hold in mind while rummaging through the antiques in **Weyburn** at the **Soo Line Historical Museum** *(3rd St. at Hwy. 39. 306-842-2922. June-Aug. Mon.-Sat., Sept.-May Mon.-Fri.; adm. fee).*

Free Land

Around the turn of the century, immigrants poured into Saskatchewan, lured by the promise of free land. "Come to me," claimed a promotional poster, "and I will give you 160 acres of land." Later settlers bought land, and even then pamphlets made it sound easy: "Pay $10.00 an acre for land within 5 miles of a railway station. Expect your land to yield 20 bushels per acre on average, and expect to receive 68 cents a bushel. Buy a good cow for $40.00. Emigrate in the spring." While 160 acres was enough for then, modern farms run over 1,000 acres.

Saskatoon North

● **540 miles/870 km** ● **4 to 5 days** ● **May to October**

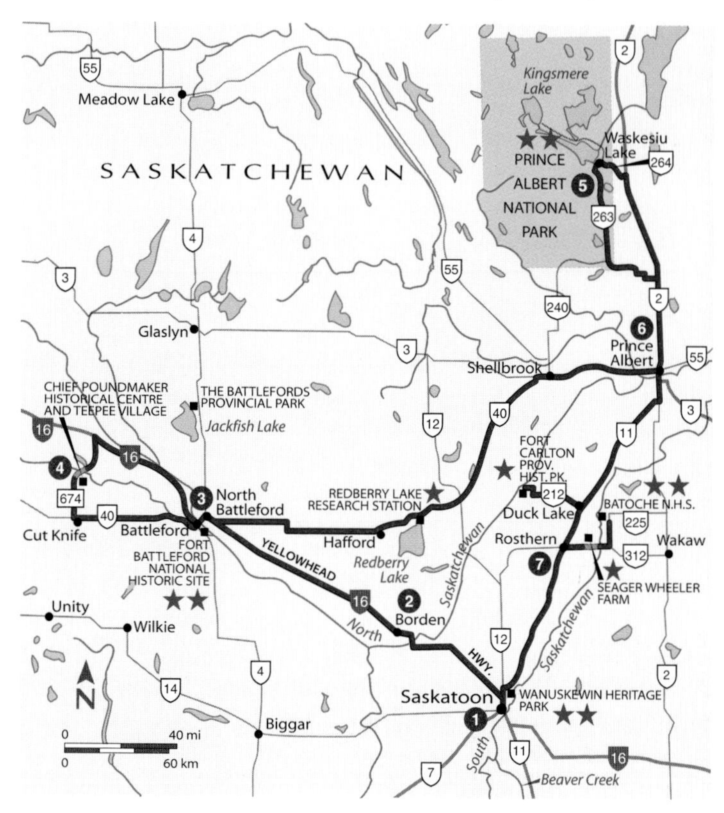

Some say Saskatchewan lacks scenery, but not if they look up at the sky, or down close to the native prairie. Nonetheless, the main theme of this drive is history, from native people to days of the fur trade to courageous settlers who built, in this great sea of space, some of the best wheat farms on earth. The route begins in Saskatoon, tracing a rough triangle to the west and north, repeatedly crossing paths with the violent and tragic events of 1885. Natural highlights include the broad valley of the North Saskatchewan River and the lakes country of Prince Albert National Park, where wolves and moose roam the boreal forest, and the northern lights overpower the stars.

The best natural feature of ❶ **Saskatoon** *(Visitor Center 306-242-1206)* is the Saskatchewan River. It says much for the wisdom of prairie folk that they have protected this waterway at the heart of their compact and openhearted city. Boasting more than 12 miles of paved pathways, numerous playgrounds, sculpture, natural areas, and other amenities, the riverfront is an almost continuous public park. Pick up maps and information at the **Meewasin Valley Centre** *(Third Ave. and 19th St. 306-665-6888).*

Visit the parks any time, but start your tour at the **Western Development Museum**★★ *(2610 Lorne Ave. S. 306-931-1910. Adm. fee).* This indoor museum re-creates a 1910 prairie town during Saskatchewan's immigration boom. Window-shop along Main Street; as you step into St. Peter's Church, the bell tolls and the organist strikes up a hymn. Walk down an alley and find yourself among steam tractors, belt-driven threshers, and binders from a time when farmers drove great puffing engines on wheels of studded steel.

Among the immigrants came thousands from Ukraine. At the **Ukrainian Museum of Canada**★ *(910 Spadina Crescent E. 306-244-3800. Closed Mon. Sept.–mid-May; adm. fee),* you'll gain an appreciation for how they got here, and the challenges they faced. For an artistic view of the prairie, drive north a few blocks to the **Mendel Art Gallery and Civic Conservatory**★ *(950 Spadina Crescent. 306-975-*

Saskatchewan River, Saskatoon

7610). Then head out to the prairie itself, for an experience that goes back long before the first plow.

Driving north on Hwy. 11, and follow signs to **Wanuskewin Heritage Park**★★ *(306-931-6767. Adm. fee).* For 6,000 years or more, native people hunted bison here, driving herds into corral-like traps or over the edge of the bluff. The way to the Visitor Center follows an actual bison "drive lane." There are no great steel machines here, but rather hide tepees, beaded clothing, stone tools, and stories told in the poetic languages of the First Nations. Exhibits tell of the people's reliance on bison, and provide excellent preparation for walking in the adjacent stream valley. Archaeological sites include a stone medicine circle, two bison jumps, and a bison pound.

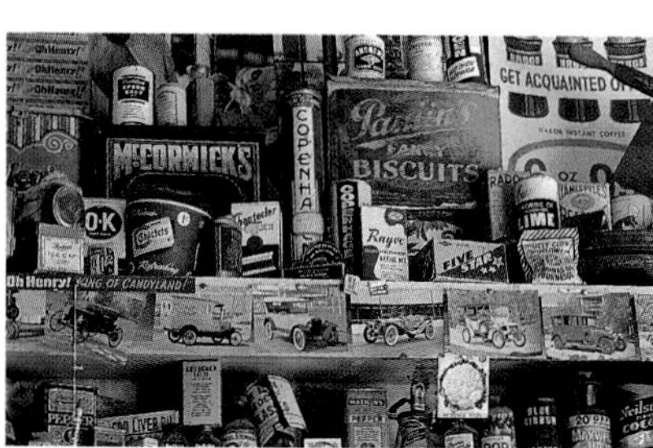

Foster's Store, Borden

Heading northwest from Saskatoon, Trans-Canada 16 meets the North Saskatchewan River as it flows through a broad, tree-lined valley. In early spring or late fall, watch for enormous white birds: This is the migrating path for endangered whooping cranes.

Take a soda break in ❷ **Borden** at **Foster's Store** *(Closed Wed. and Sun.),* an old general store still operating and crammed with things that might have been sold decades ago. Old-fashioned remedies and knickknacks (not for sale) jam the shelves beside modern goods.

First Nations

While the terms Native American and Indian are widely used throughout the United States, the name First Nations is more commonly employed when referring to Canada's original peoples. However, since that name does not include the Inuit—Eskimo people—or the Métis—descendants of Indians and European fur traders—the term Aboriginal is frequently used when referring to all native groups. Canadians do not consider the word derogatory or offensive.

In ❸ **North Battleford,** step back to the 1920s at a second **Western Development Museum★★** *(Trans-Canada 16 and Hwy. 40. 306-445-8033. April-Dec.; adm. fee).* Past a small but good collection of early cars comes an exhibit titled "The Jolly Life of a Farmer's Wife," detailing the farm household of the 1920s, when most implements were still woman-powered. Outside, more than 30 buildings re-create a prairie village complete with houses, shops, churches, and a grain elevator. The barbershop includes what looks to be a torture device: the Helene Curtis Tru-Art Permanent Wave Machine, its 32 curling irons hanging from heavy cords around a bizarre headpiece.

Across Trans-Canada 16, the **George Hooey Wildlife Collection** *(Wildlife Federation Bldg. 306-445-4244. July-Aug. Mon.-Fri.; donation)* contains mounted wildlife. In town, the **Allen Sapp Gallery★** *(1 Railway Ave. 306-445-1760. Closed Mon.-Tues. Oct.-May; donation)* shows the simple, eloquent work of Mr. Sapp, a local Cree and one of Canada's most celebrated painters. If military uniforms, mustache cups, and firearms are of interest, cross the river to the older community of **Battleford** and the **Fred Light Museum** *(Central Ave. and 20th St. 306-937-7111. Mid-May–Labor Day; donation).*

History still breathes down the road at **Fort Battleford National Historic Site★★** *(S on Central Ave. 306-937-2621. Mid-May–mid-Oct.; adm. fee).* A former post of the North

West Mounted Police, its most dramatic moment came in 1885, when Métis and Cree rebels took up arms in a dispute with the federal government and fearful settlers crowded into the flimsy stockade. Today a few original buildings survive and guides in period costume interpret the life of a Mountie on what was then the frontier.

From Battleford, take Hwy. 40 through rolling hills to the town of **Cut Knife,** which claims the world's largest tomahawk *(Tomahawk Park).* The adjacent **Clayton McLain Memorial Museum**★ *(306-398-2590. July-Aug.; adm. fee)* is more interesting, if only for the poignancy of personal objects. Labels give the family history of items including wedding dresses, photo albums, toys, and other artifacts.

To get the native view of the 1885 resistance, visit the ❹ **Chief Poundmaker Historical Centre and Teepee**

Paddleboats at The Battlefords Provincial Park

Village *(N on Rte. 674, follow signs. 306-398-8044. May–Sept.; adm. fee).* The Visitor Center, situated on the hill where the battle was fought in 1885, displays photos and handicrafts, but few artifacts—it is ironic that the Poundmaker Cree Nation possesses so few historical items for its own museum. Even Poundmaker's sacred bundle is owned by others; it rests in a glass case at the museum in Cut Knife.

If swimming or bird-watching sounds appealing, venture north to Jackfish Lake and **The Battlefords Provincial Park** *(306-386-2212. Adm. fee).* Set among wooded coulees and exposed prairie ridges, the park offers a beach, golf course, lodge, campsites, and trails.

Old barn south of Hwy. 40, near Redberry Lake

Early Transport

Over the years, Fort Carlton saw many types of transport. From 1810 to 1860, York boats plied the North Saskatchewan River on their way between Hudson Bay and Fort Edmonton. After 1859, when the railroad brought freight as far as St. Paul, Minnesota, goods came overland on Red River carts—effective vehicles but notorious for their ungreased, squeaking axles. For a while, steamships operated between Lake Winnipeg and the Rocky Mountains, but the rivers proved treacherous. It was a big day when the railroad finally crossed the prairie.

Returning to Battleford, drive east on Hwy. 40 past Hafford to the **Redberry Lake Research Station★** *(306-549-2400. Call for schedule).* Here, displays and spotting scopes focus on an island nesting colony of white pelicans.

Continue on Hwy. 40 to Shellbrook and Prince Albert. Before exploring the town, head north on Hwy. 2 and Hwy. 263 into the whispering forests of ❺ **Prince Albert National Park★★** *(306-663-5322. Adm. fee).* Located in the transition zone between the aspen forests and the vast boreal forests of the north, it spans both realms. Loons call on quiet lakes. Wolves and elk leave tracks on sandy lake shores. And the aurora borealis hangs eerily in the night sky, sometimes mixing its glow with the flash of lightning from distant thunderstorms. **Waskesiu Lake** townsite provides services, but the park's natural beauty is best experienced away from the resort atmosphere. Look for deer and foxes along scenic **Kingsmere Road,** consider a camping trip on the Bagwa canoe route, or simply walk the **Waskesiu River Nature Trail,** a boardwalk accessible to wheelchairs. If you sit quietly, this marshy area comes alive with kingfishers diving for minnows, herons stalking the reeds, and beavers drifting through the shadows.

Return to ❻ **Prince Albert** *(Visitor Center 306-953-4385),* along the North Saskatchewan River. The province's oldest continuously settled agricultural community, it began as a Presbyterian mission in 1866. Explore its history at the **Prince Albert Historical Museum★** *(River St. at Central Ave. 306-764-2992. Mid-May–Labor Day; adm. fee),* in the old brick fire station, an attraction in itself. Or tap into electioneering at the **Diefenbaker House Museum** *(246 19th St. W. 306-953-4863. Mid-May–Labor Day; donation),* former home of John Diefenbaker, prime minister from 1957 to 1963.

Pick up the thread of the Métis Resistance again to the south at the **Duck Lake Regional Interpretive Centre**★ *(Anderson Ave., Duck Lake. 306-467-2057. Mid-May–Sept.; adm. fee).* The collection includes Gabriel Dumont's watch and the original letter Louis Riel wrote to his mother the night before his hanging. Other items illustrate life in the area over the past century. The center is complemented by the murals painted on buildings throughout town.

If you have a sack of dried bison meat with you, trade for blankets at **Fort Carlton Provincial Historic Park**★ *(Hwy. 212. 306-467-4512. Mid-May–Labor Day; adm. fee),* the partial reconstruction of a Hudson's Bay Company provisioning post and transport hub. Between 1810 and 1885, York boats, Red River carts, packtrains, dogsleds, and even steamships passed this way carrying goods up and down the North Saskatchewan. As its last act, Fort Carlton played a role in the events of 1885, which ignited when police from the fort confronted Métis and native men near Duck Lake.

More of the story is told at **Batoche National Historic Site**★★ *(15 mi/24 km NE of Rosthern via Hwy. 225. 306-423-6227. Mid-May–mid-Oct.; adm. fee).* The audiovisual show is exceptional, coloring your feelings as you tour the surviving buildings of this former Métis settlement and battlefield. At its center is 1896 **St. Antoine de Padoue** church and rectory.

Exhibit at Prince Albert Historical Museum

On the road back to Rosthern, drop in for iced tea and fresh Saskatoon-berry pie at the **Seager Wheeler Farm**★ *(Hwy. 312 E of Rosthern. 306-232-5959. Mid-May–Labor Day; adm. fee),* home of world-famous wheat farmer Seager Wheeler. The pioneering techniques that won him international awards are illustrated by exhibits and by the farm itself, now being restored to its 1919 condition, along with extensive rose gardens.

Finally, have a last brush with treasures from the past in ❼ **Rosthern,** where the **Mennonite Heritage Museum** *(510 6th Ave. 306-232-4415. April-Sept. Sat.-Sun.; adm. fee)* contains at least one that should stay there: the Celebrated Healer Home Electric Shock Treatment Machine.

Calgary and Dinosaurs★★

● 750 miles/1,200 km ● 5 to 6 days ● May through September

This sensational, remarkably diverse journey through southwestern Alberta combines the big city pleasures of Calgary and the dazzling alpine scenery of the Canadian Rockies with a fascinating excursion into the world of the dinosaurs. After taking in Calgary's rich assortment of museums, the route flirts with the heights among the coal-mining towns of Crowsnest Pass and the blocky summits of Waterton Lakes National Park. It then bowls east across the plains before heading north to explore dinosaur bone beds and the fabulous Royal Tyrrell Museum of Palaeontology—perhaps the finest dinosaur museum in the world.

Initially a lonely outpost for the red-coated North West Mounted Police, ❶ **Calgary** *(Visitor Center 403-263-8510 or*

800-661-1678) is a sprawling, modern city at the western fringe of the Great Plains. Full of excellent museums, site of the 1988 Winter Olympics, and home to one of the west's wildest rodeos, Calgary lies within sight of the Rocky Mountains and boasts a generous network of parks and greenbelts along its rivers.

It all started in 1875 when the Mounties built a fort at the confluence of the Bow and Elbow Rivers, to help bring law and order to the Canadian west. Today, at **Fort Calgary Historic Park★** *(750 Ninth Ave. S.E. 403-290-1875. May–early Oct.; adm. fee),* the log-palisaded fort is being rebuilt on its original site. Walk through the fort, then drop by the interpretive center to learn about the Mounties' mission and lives.

"Brotherhood of Mankind" statues, Calgary

Nearby, the **Calgary Zoo, Botanical Garden and Prehistoric Park** *(1300 Zoo Rd. 403-232-9300. Adm. fee)* houses 1,200 animals from around the world, extensive gardens, and dinosaur reproductions in a Mesozoic Alberta setting.

Downtown, the **Glenbow Museum, Art Gallery, Library and Archives★★** *(130 Ninth Ave. S.E. 403-268-4100. Closed Mon. mid-Oct.–mid-May; adm. fee)* offers a marvelous overview of western Canada's rich cultural heritage, from the traditional lives of First Nations peoples to the polyglot of European immigrants who settled in Alberta during the 1880s. Nearby, hands-on changing exhibits at the **Calgary Science Centre★** *(701 11th St. S.W. 403-221-3700. Adm. fee)* provide interactive and entertaining science lessons, as well as a huge dome-shaped screen offering an exhilarating film or star show.

Northwest of downtown **Canada Olympic Park★★** *(Trans-Canada 1. 403-247-5452)* lies on a grassy ridge overlooking Calgary. In 1988 the world's finest ski jumpers,

Indoor Oasis

Are you in Calgary and in the mood for a picnic even though it's sleeting? Brown-bag it at **Devonian Gardens** *(Toronto Dominion Square, 4th floor, 317 Seventh Ave. S.W. 403-268-3830)*, a lush, 2.5-acre indoor park with ponds, waterfalls, bridges, and a playground.

Canada Olympic Park, Calgary

luge riders, and bobsled teams competed here. The **Olympic Hall of Fame** *(Fee)* tells the history of the games. Outside, strap on a helmet and ride a luge *(summer only; fee),* or bobsled *(winter only; fee),* or watch ski jumpers fling themselves from the 70-meter tower—even in summer.

On Calgary's near south side, you'll find the **Museum of the Regiments★★** *(4520 Crowchild Trail S.W. 403-240-7057. Thurs.-Tues.; donation),* a first-rate military museum tracking four Canadian regiments from formation to recent peacekeeping missions. Actual-size dioramas of battle scenes, vintage tanks, guns, swords, maps, flags, and other exhibits show the human cost of combat.

For a vivid glimpse of life in western Canada from 1860 to 1914, continue south to **Heritage Park★★** *(1900 Heritage Dr. S.W. 403-259-1900. Daily late May–early Sept., Sat.-Sun. early Sept.–early Oct.; adm. fee),* a 66-acre park with dozens of restored or replicated buildings, an antique midway, and hundreds of costumed interpreters eager to talk your ear off.

Luge run, Canada Olympic Park

Out by the airport, admire gleaming vintage aircraft and watch restoration work in progress at the **Aero Space Museum★** *(4629 McCall Way N.E. 403-250-3752. Adm. fee).* Elsewhere, stroll along the Bow River at one of two excellent parks: **Inglewood Bird Sanctuary** *(Ninth Ave. and Sanctuary Rd. S.E. 403-269-6688),* with sightings of 250 species of birds; or **Fish Creek Provincial Park** *(15979 Bull Bottom Trail S.E. 403-297-5293),* with its coyote dens and heron colony.

Follow Hwy. 2 south to **High River** and tour restored locomotive and railroad cars at the **Museum of the Highwood** *(406 First St. 403-652-7156. Closed Mon. Labor Day–*

mid-May; adm. fee). Then take Rte. 543 west across the **Highwood River,** a fine trout stream, and follow Hwy. 22 south to ❷ **Bar U Ranch National Historic Site★★** *(403-395-2212. Fee for tours).* Established in 1882 as headquarters for an immense open-range ranch, the site takes in 35 buildings. Most await restoration, but excellent guides present a clear picture of ranching in general and of those who labored here.

Continue south to Hwy. 3 (Crowsnest Hwy.), turning west toward the blocky crest of the Canadian Rockies and **Crowsnest Pass★,** revered for its scenery but remembered more as the site of several coal-mining disasters and a colossal landslide. After the railroad built a branch line over the pass in 1897, a string of coal mines and company towns sprang up. Walk through the roofless, sandstone powerhouse of one such mine, **Leitch Collieries** *(Hwy. 3. 403-562-7388. Tours in summer; donation),* and learn about the work of miners, as well as the crews that braced the tunnels, supplied fresh air, and manned the long row of nearby coke ovens.

Bar U Ranch National Historic Site

Farther up the road, don a hard hat and step into the startling chill and darkness of the **Bellevue Underground Mine★** *(Off Hwy. 3, Bellevue. 403-562-7388. Tours mid-May–early Sept., and by appt.; adm. fee),* active from 1903 to 1962. A coal dust explosion here in 1910 killed 30 miners, but it was by no means the area's worst accident. Across the road, at **Hillcrest Cemetery,** lie the mass graves of 189 men killed in a 1914 explosion in the Hillcrest Mine.

The highway soon winds through acres of limestone rubble that peeled away from Turtle Mountain on April 29, 1903, obliterating much of the town of Frank and killing at least 70 people. The **Frank Slide Interpretive Centre★** *(403-562-7388. Adm. fee)* faces the vast scar on Turtle Mountain and overlooks the 82 million tons of rock and debris. Exhibits tell the dramatic story of the catastrophe.

Double back to Pincher Creek and turn south toward ❸ **Waterton Lakes National Park★★** *(Hwy. 5. 403-859-22024. Adm. fee),* where the rolling Great Plains end abruptly against the Canadian Rockies. An extraordinary landscape of towering cliffs, plunging waterfalls, large mountain lakes, broad valleys, and swift icy streams, Waterton is home of a large variety of birds and wildlife.

Entering the park, look for hawks gliding over the prairie meadows, then visit the **Bison Paddock,** where 12 to 20 plains bison live in a large, grassy enclosure. Farther along the main road, drop by the **Prince of Wales Hotel**★★ *(403-236-3400),* a gorgeous gingerbread lodge built in 1927. Its rustic lobby overlooks **Upper Waterton Lake,** which sprawls beneath soaring 8,000-foot peaks and extends south into Glacier National Park in Montana. Pick up maps and advice at the Visitor Center across the road, and con-

Early morning view, Prince of Wales Hotel, Waterton Lakes National Park

sider a guided hike up the nearby **Bear's Hump Trail**★, which offers an even better view of the upper valley.

For a less strenuous jaunt, head for **Waterton Park** townsite and its shaded lakeshore paths. You're likely to see mule deer and bighorn sheep cropping people's shrubs. Get a quick rundown on the park's natural history at the **Heritage Centre** *(Waterton Ave.)* and think about a half-day cruise *(Waterton Inter-Nation Shoreline Cruises 403-859-2362. Fare)* to **Goat Haunt,** in Glacier National Park.

Next, follow the winding Akamina Parkway into deep subalpine forest surrounding **Cameron Lake,** a small alpine jewel glimmering beneath a cirque of high cliffs. To tour the park's third major valley, go back to Middle

Waterton Lake and follow Blackiston Creek through expansive meadows to **Red Rock Canyon★,** an incredible chasm of smooth pink rock cut by a stream of sapphire water. Bighorn sheep frequent this area. Scan the open valley floor and grassy mountain slopes for bear, deer, and elk.

From Waterton, Hwy. 5 descends across prairie foothills to **Cardston** and the **Remington-Alberta Carriage Centre★★** *(623 Main St. 403-653-5139. Adm. fee),* a first-rate museum devoted to horse-drawn conveyances in all their abundant varieties. Interpreted with intelligence and wit, the museum offers much more than a fabulous collection of restored vehicles. It also explains how these beautiful objects were designed and built, what they were created for, and how the horses and drivers were trained.

Head north on Hwy. 2 to ❹ **Fort Macleod** *(Chamber of Commerce 403-553-4955),* established in 1874 as the first outpost of the North West Mounted Police. A copy of a log-palisaded compound houses the **Fort Museum★** *(219 25th St. 403-553-4703. Daily May–mid-Oct., Mon.-Fri. mid-Oct.–Dec. and March-April; adm. fee),* jammed with Red Coat memorabilia as well as pioneer and native artifacts.

West of town, **Head-Smashed-In Buffalo Jump★★** *(Rte. 785. 403-553-2731. Adm. fee)* preserves one of the oldest, largest, and least disturbed bison-kill sites in North America. For at least 5,000 years, hunters on foot stampeded herds of bison over this long band of sandstone cliffs, then butchered them with stone tools. Excellent exhibits cover the lifestyle of these prehistoric peoples and explain the hunt in detail—from preparatory ceremonies to the manifold uses for bison meat, bone, hide, horn, and sinew. Self-guided trails loop past the kill site.

Perched above the Oldman River, **Lethbridge** *(Visitor Center 403-320-1222)* has grown from an 1880s coal-mining and railroading town into Alberta's third largest city. Before then, in 1869, American traders built a fort beside the river and began trading whiskey for buffalo robes. Today, a convincing replica of the notorious **Fort Whoop-Up★** *(West and 3rd Aves. 403-329-0444. Adm. fee)* stands at **Indian Battle Park.** Well-stocked with fur-trade items, it chronicles the depressing history of the whiskey trade, which led to the demise of both bison and Blackfeet, and prompted the formation of the North West Mounted Police. The park takes its name from North America's last major intertribal battle, held here in 1870, in which some 350 Cree and

Mule deer and fawns, Waterton Lakes National Park

Windy Waterton

Famous as a windy place, Waterton Lakes National Park often shudders under gusts of 75 miles per hour and has recorded wind speeds of 100 mph. In 1927, while the Prince of Wales Hotel was under construction, ferocious blasts pushed the completed timber frame along its foundation two separate times. The hotel has never been square since.

Overlook, Dinosaur Provincial Park

Blackfeet died. Nearby, the **Helen Schuler Coulee Centre** *(Third Ave. and Scenic Dr. S. 403-320-3064. Closed Mon. Sept.-May)* interprets the region's ecology. Elsewhere, stroll through traditional Japanese landscaping and architecture at the **Nikka Yuko Japanese Garden** *(Mayor Magrath Dr. at Henderson Lake. 403-328-3511. Mid-May–Labor Day; adm. fee),* and brush up on Lethbridge history at the **Sir Alexander Galt Museum** *(W end of Fifth Ave. S. 403-320-3898).*

For a chance to see a trained falcon streak over the grass at 60 mph, continue east on Hwy. 3 to **Coaldale** and the **Alberta Birds of Prey Centre** *(2124 Burrowing Owl Lane. 800-661-1222. May-Sept.; adm. fee),* which rehabilitates and releases injured hawks, owls, falcons, and eagles.

Hwy. 4 leads southeast to ❺ **Warner.** Here **Devil's Coulee Dinosaur Egg Site Interpretive Centre**★ *(403-642-2118. Daily mid-May–Labor Day, Mon.-Wed. rest of year; donation)* runs two-hour tours of a phenomenal dinosaur nesting site, where scientists have unearthed fossilized eggs containing complete, embryonic skeletons. Or spend a day or a week digging in the badlands with a paleontologist.

Northeast, among the contorted badlands beyond Brooks, lies one of the world's preeminent deposits of Cretaceous dinosaur bones. Protected and made partially accessible to the public by ❻ **Dinosaur Provincial Park**★★ *(403-378-4342. Adm. fee),* the area contains more than 200 bone beds yielding the remains of more than 35 species of dinosaurs, along with crocodiles, turtles, fish, lizards, flying reptiles, and small mammals. Most of the fossils are taken elsewhere, but the **Field Station Visitor Centre**★ *(Tours mid-May–mid-Oct.; adm. fee)* displays

Writing-on-Stone★

Consider a side trip to **Writing-On-Stone Provincial Park**★ *(26 miles/42 km E of Milk River on Rte. 501. 403-547-2364. May–Labor Day),* which preserves a large concentration of native petroglyphs and pictographs in a compelling prairie landscape of sandstone cliffs and oddly shaped pillars called hoodoos. The finest examples lie within a restricted area accessible only during guided hikes, but you can reach the Battle Scene, a 250-character petroglyph, on your own.

several examples, including a magnificent hunting scene with a pack of small, agile carnivores pulling down a large hadrosaur (duckbill). It's a terrific museum, but most visitors come for the excellent interpretive tours that explore the restricted area by bus and on foot. The park also runs tours of the lab where scientists prepare and assemble fossils. Tours sell out early, but five self-guided trails and two fossil display buildings are open year-round.

Return to Trans-Canada 1, jog northwest and follow Hwy. 56 north to the Drumheller Valley, where 139 coal mines once dotted the hills above the Red Deer River. In **East Coulee,** visit the **Historic Atlas Coal Mine** *(Hwy. 10. 403-822-2220. Mid-May–mid-Oct.; adm. fee),* with its weathered 1937 wooden tipple, mining machinery, and miner's shack. While in 7 **Drumheller,** set aside at least a few hours to visit the astonishing **Royal Tyrrell Museum of Palaeontology**★★ *(N. Dinosaur Trail, NW of Drumheller via Hwy. 10. 403-823-7707. Closed Mon. mid-Oct.–mid-May; adm. fee).* Probably the finest dinosaur museum in the world, this sprawling, creative, intensely engaging place sketches the evolution of life from algal slime to *Homo sapiens,* but devotes most of its space and attention to dinosaurs. Nothing conveys the scale of these colossal animals quite like fully articulated skeletons, and here you wander among three dozen. There's a complete *Tyrannosaurus rex* (one of fewer than ten in the world), as well as other predators, an array of plant eaters, and many marine and flying reptiles. None of these stand as passive displays. Many suggest motion, while others illustrate the process of excavation, or serve as riddles mulled over by videotaped paleontologists. All wait amid imaginative exhibits covering such topics as skin texture, coloration, tactics for hunting and defense, and the competing theories for why they became extinct. The Tyrrell also offers tours of a fossil site and opportunties to dig alongside a paleontologist.

Albertosaurus, Royal Tyrrell Museum of Palaeontology

Return to Calgary via Hwy. 9.

Park Circle★★

● 760 miles/1,225 km ● 6 to 7 days ● June to September ● Do not expect to find a vacant campsite in Banff or Jasper National Parks after 4 p.m. ● Visit popular sites before 10 a.m. to avoid crowds.

Starting on the fringe of the Great Plains and climbing through the incomparable mountain scenery of Banff and Jasper National Parks, this magnificent drive combines exhilarating vistas of forest, crag, and glacier with some of the finest museums and historic sites in western Canada. Rodeo, art, the fur trade, Ukrainian heritage, death-feigning beetles, and two subspecies of bison—all this and more help maintain a keen interest in one's surroundings long after the peaks slip from view. The route begins near Calgary, making a broad loop that stretches north through the mountains before turning east to Edmonton.

Grizzly bear, Banff National Park

From Calgary (p. 112), follow Hwy. 1A northwest to ❶ **Cochrane,** an old ranching town at the foot of the Rockies and now a Calgary bedroom community. Little of the cowboy era remains at **Cochrane Ranche Provincial Historic Site** *(Jct. of Hwys. 22 and 1A. 403-932-2909. June-Aug.),* headquarters for Alberta's first large-scale ranch—a 189,000-acre flop, founded in 1881.

Other ranches thrived, of course, and the **Western Heritage Center**★ *(403-932-3514. Adm. fee),* just north, celebrates both failures and triumphs with imaginative interactive displays, an art gallery, and an excellent Rodeo Hall of Fame.

To the west, Hwy. 1A weaves through prairie foothills and climbs along the Bow River to Trans-Canada 1 and

Moraine Lake, Banff National Park

on into the forest and grand interior mountain valleys of Canada's first national park, **Banff National Park**★★ *(Visitor Center 403-762-1550. Adm. fee),* established in 1885. Stretching roughly 250 miles (400 km) along the jagged crest of the Canadian Rockies, Banff and the adjoining Jasper National Park take in a vast tangle of great strapping peaks, mauled by glaciers and capped by the largest ice fields south of Alaska. Meltwaters thunder from the heights, pool in gemlike alpine lakes, and rush down the forested walls of broad U-shaped valleys into powerful rivers. It's a staggering, heart-swelling landscape, rich in wildlife, laced with hiking trails, and traversed by the most spectacular system of roads in the Rockies.

An 1880s railroad town and tourist destination from the start, ❷ **Banff**★ *(Visitor Center 403-762-8421)* lies along the Bow River in a broad valley ringed with forested peaks that dwarf a crush of hotels, restaurants, and shops. The dense evergreen trees, swift blue waters of the Bow, and an abundance of bike trails, picnic spots, and footpaths mitigate the traffic and help Banff avoid the carnival air that can mar national park gateways.

For a quick summary of Banff's human history, visit the

Banff's Elk

Spotting wildlife is never a sure thing, but some good bets for seeing elk near Banff include: the **Fenland Trail**, a 1.2-mile path along a marsh east of town on the Mount Norquay Road; the **Indian Grounds**, an open grassy area east of town along Banff Ave.; the **Cave and Basin** lawns early in the morning; and **Backswamp**, 2 miles (3.2 km) west on the Bow Valley Parkway.

What to do in Banff

Interpretive programs at Banff and Jasper include guided hikes and strolls, campfire chats, and theater presentations. Tickets must be purchased at park Visitor Centers for most, but not all, of the programs. In the Banff area, look for two-to-three-hour walks among the Vermilion Lakes, along the shore of Lake Minnewanka, and up the flanks of Tunnel Mountain. Near Lake Louise, outings range from a two-hour jaunt along the shoreline, to six-hour hikes to the Plain of Six Glaciers area and the Valley of the Ten Peaks. In Jasper enjoy an evening presentation about the park at the Whistlers Outdoor Theater, or a campfire chat at Wabasso Campground. Guided walks include a tour of Jasper's historic buildings, and a trip to see beaver in Cottonwood Slough.

Whyte Museum of the Canadian Rockies★ *(111 Bear St. 403-762-2291. Closed Mon. mid-Oct.–late May; adm. fee),* which bridges the 10,000-year gulf between those who hunted huge Pleistocene mountain sheep with chert spearpoints and the Victorian gents who tackled the same peaks in waistcoats and ties. Nearby, western Canada's oldest natural history museum, the rustic 1903 **Banff Park Museum★** *(91 Banff Ave. 403-762-1558. Adm. fee)* remains true to its era with stuffed specimens of moose, bears, bison, foxes, and dozens of birds displayed in elegant glass-fronted cabinets.

Across the river stands the park's **Administration Building★,** a noble stone facade reminiscent of an English country house and surrounded by expansive lawns, rock grottoes, and terraced gardens. While you're in the area, stop at the **Luxton Museum** *(1 Birch Ave. 403-762-2388. Closed Mon.-Tues. Nov.-March; adm. fee)* to admire the handiwork of various native peoples. Next, follow Cave Avenue west through the forest to the birthplace of Canada's national park system, **Cave and Basin National Historic Site★★** *(403-762-1557. Adm. fee),* where two hot springs bubble to the surface—one inside a cave, the other nestled against the hillside—both within a restored 1914 native stone bathing complex. Duck through a low tunnel into the cave, with its wide pool of clear sulfurous water. Outdoors, admire the view from the reflecting pond, and peer into the colorful waters of the basin. Exhibits explain how this compelling spot led to the establishment of Banff.

Since swimming is no longer allowed at Cave and Basin, follow Mountain Avenue to **Upper Hot Springs** *(403-762-1515. Adm. fee),* where a historic stone bathhouse and outdoor pool face the tilted gray slabs of Mount Rundle. Nearby, the **Sulphur Mountain Gondola** *(403-762-5438. Call for schedule; fare)* climbs 2,292 vertical feet to a summit restaurant, trails, and knockout alpine vistas.

Back in Banff, follow Birch Avenue east to **Bow Falls,** then drive up to the 1928 **Banff Springs Hotel★★** *(End of Spray Ave. 403-762-2211. Fee for tours, offered daily in summer).* Pick up a map in the lobby and wander through this colossal stone palace—rustic, elegant, and a bit medieval. In 1941 a week of room, board, and golf, plus a round-trip first-class train ticket from San Francisco, cost $145.75.

Northeast of Banff, follow the 9-mile (14-km) loop road past **Lake Minnewanka★,** an immense, fjordlike lake cradled between massive peaks, and explore the remains of **Bankhead,** an old coal-mining town. Then head north on the **Bow Valley Parkway.** A slower, quieter route than Trans-Canada 1, it still delivers you to Lake Louise in about an hour, offering better views of the mountains and a far better chance of seeing elk, deer, coyotes, and bears.

Along the way, hike up **Johnston Canyon★★** *(11 mi/ 18 km NW of Banff),* a narrow limestone chasm with two thundering waterfalls. Crowded but worth it, the spectacular 1.6-mile trail veers out over the rushing water on catwalks bolted to the cliffs. It also offers the rare opportunity of standing beside the very base of an immensely powerful falls, amid the blast and spray and percussive, gut-thumping crash of exploding white water.

Along the Bow Valley Parkway

To reach **Lake Louise★★,** follow Hwy. 1A past the Lake Louise townsite, cross the river, and climb through steep subalpine forests to the jammed parking areas below **Chateau Lake Louise★** *(403-522-3511),* a massive, cream-colored edifice walling off the eastern lakeshore. Rubberneck the lobby, then amble out to the mobbed shoreline. The lake itself stretches off between high, knobby peaks to the abrupt wall of glacier-clad Mount Victoria, which soars 11,365 feet. Take the shoreline path to the end of the lake and back (2.5 miles), or hike up to the teahouse at **Plain of Six Glaciers** (7 miles).

Follow the cutoff to **Moraine Lake★★,** a luminescent turquoise gem nestled beneath a long row of crumbling summits that form the **Valley of the Ten Peaks★.**

Back in town, stop by the **Lake Louise Visitor Centre** *(403-522-3833)* for a geology summary of the Canadian Rockies. Out back, you'll find the start of the **Bow River Trail,** a 4.4-mile interpretive loop. For a grandstand vista of the glacier-capped peaks, glide up the flanks of Mount Whitehorn on the **Lake Louise Sightseeing Lift & Gondola★** *(403-522-3555. June–late Sept.; fare).*

Most people find it hard to tear away from Lake Louise, but a great swath of sensational country awaits north

Chateau Lake Louise

along the **Icefields Parkway★★** *(Hwy. 93),* Canada's highest road. Named for the hundred-plus glaciers visible along the route, the parkway bowls along for 143 miles (230 km), passing through long, forested river valleys cradled by nearly continuous walls of dazzling peaks. Drivers frequently spot elk, moose, bighorn sheep, mountain goats, and black bears. A lucky few see a grizzly, wolf, or caribou. After about 20 miles (32 km) of forest and crag, pull over beside **Bow Lake** for a good look at **Crowfoot Glacier★** clinging to the scabrous cliffs of Crowfoot Mountain. From the lake's north end, you can make out **Bow Glacier Falls,** a ferocious cascade plummeting nearly 500 feet. A 3-mile trail leads to its base.

At **Bow Summit,** follow the spur road west and stroll to where **Peyto Lake Viewpoint★** overlooks a creamy blue lake, its glacial source, and the broad, forested valley of the Mistaya River. Continue past **Upper** and **Lower Waterfowl Lakes,** and walk down to **Mistaya Canyon★,** a sinuous fissure so narrow and deep you may have trouble seeing the water that crashes through it.

At Saskatchewan River Crossing, pick up the gravelly bed of the **North Saskatchewan River** and begin a climb toward the treeless alpine zone. Not far beyond the **Weeping Wall** (the damp brow of curving limestone to your right), the road makes a sharp curve and begins a steep ascent. As you round its northern flank, consider hiking to the crest of **Parker Ridge★,** a fairly strenuous climb to a panoramic vista of the **Saskatchewan Glacier,** curving down from the edge of the vast **Columbia Icefield.**

Soon you cross **Sunwapta Pass** into **Jasper National Park★★** *(Visitor Center 403-852-6176. Adm. fee),* descending to the toe of **Athabasca Glacier★★,** a broad ramp of ice and snow slanting down between **Mount Athabasca** (left) and **Snow Dome.** Signs along the spur road record the pace of its retreat during the past hundred years. Hike to the edge of the glacier, but don't venture onto the ice without a qualified guide—the crevasses are deep, and people have died in them recently.

Across the highway, learn about glacial mechanics at the **Icefield Centre★★,** a thronged activity complex where you can grab a bite, book a Snocoach tour of the glacier, or visit the best natural history museum in either park. A large three-dimensional projection of the Columbia Icefield clearly shows its extent (125 square miles) and its three meltwater drainages (Arctic, Atlantic, Pacific). Other displays examine wildlife of the alpine zone and explain how glaciers form, grow, and retreat.

Follow the Sunwapta River northwest as it rushes down into the forest and gathers strength from countless creeks and waterfalls spilling from the **Winston Churchill Range** to the west. Peer over the cliffs at **Sunwapta Falls★,** a great ripping blast of foam, then coast along the Athabasca River to the **Mounts Fryatt, Brussels, and Christie Viewpoint★★.** Perched on a natural mineral lick, this is one of the park's most dependable sites for spotting mountain goats. Next, turn onto Hwy. 93A and take in **Athabasca Falls★★,** always crowded, and for good reason. Here, the river's milky blue waters funnel into a chasm and break into a creamy plume of white water with Mount Kerkeslin as a backdrop. Several miles farther north, take the slow, 9-mile (14-km) side trip to the base of **Mount Edith Cavell★★,** a vast wall of dark gray rock and snow that sweeps upward nearly a vertical mile from the parking area. **Angel Glacier** spills from the cliffs like an immense petrified waterfall, and two short loop trails beckon.

Then it's on to Banff's northern counterpart, ❸ **Jasper** *(Visitor Center 403-852-3858),* a turn-of-the-century railroad town and resort area that lies along the Athabasca River within sight of four mountain ranges. Small lakes—some

The Icefields

Roadbound travelers rarely see more than the tantalizing fringe of the vast Columbia Icefields—usually as a serpentine glacier clinging to the cliffs, sometimes as a noble valley glacier plowing down between the flanks of the mountains. Replenished with 23 feet of new snow each year (on average), the largest body of ice in the Rockies covers 125 square miles with ice that reaches a maximum depth of 1,200 feet.

warm enough for a dip—dot the valley floor, and trails for walking and biking loop throughout.

For an aerial view, board the **Jasper Tramway★★** *(S of town off Hwy. 93. 403-852-3093. April-Oct.; fare),* soar over the steep northern face of **The Whistlers,** and walk a short distance to the summit through wildflowers. Jasper lies 4,300 feet below, the Columbia Icefield shines to the south, and you might catch a glimpse of Mount Robson to the west. The view can leave you stammering.

Maligne Canyon

Northeast of town, **Maligne Canyon★★** *(Follow signs off Trans-Canada 16)* cuts across the forest floor as a deep, serpentine crack where the Maligne (muh-LAYN) River slips, pools, swerves, and drops among potholes, hollows, and smooth overhanging walls of limestone. Loiter or hike along the brink, then continue beside the river past **Medicine Lake★** to **Maligne Lake★★,** the region's longest (13.8 miles) and deepest (318 feet). Book a 90-minute cruise *(Maligne Tours 403-852-3370. May-Sept.; reservations advised; fare)* and glide down this narrow lake toward the bulky, glaciated peaks that crowd its southern shore.

If there's time, consider a half-day side trip into **Mount Robson Provincial Park** *(55 mi/88.5 km W on Trans-Canada 16. 604-566-4325)* to see 12,972-foot **Mount Robson★★,** the highest peak in the Canadian Rockies, and a stunner even after you've grown blasé about mountains.

Near the park border, as you head east to leave Jasper behind, take the turnoff for **Miette Hot Springs★** *(403-866-3939. May-Oct.; adm. fee),* a steaming outdoor pool in the mountains. Along the way, peer into **Punchbowl Falls,** a thin veil of white water slipping into a chasm Henry Moore might have designed. Return to Trans-Canada 16 and descend eastward out onto the prairies. Near Edmonton, take Hwy. 2 north to **St. Albert** *(Visitor Center 403-459-1724),* established as a Catholic mission and farm town in the 1860s. At **Father Lacombe Chapel Provincial Historic Site★** *(St. Vital Ave. W of St. Albert Trail.*

403-427-2022. Mid-May–Labor Day; adm. fee), step into Alberta's oldest standing building—a square-hewn log chapel, built in 1861 and restored. Next door, track missionary history at the 1887 **Bishop Grandin Residence.**

Alberta's capital city, ❹ **Edmonton** *(Visitor Center 403-496-8400 or 800-463-4667),* is a large, sprawling urban center divided by a sinuous oasis of shady parks stretching along the North Saskatchewan River. Established in 1795 as a fur-trading post, it became a permanent settlement during the 1870s and thrived as the farm, ranch, and petroleum industries boomed around it.

If for nothing more than anthropological curiosity, have a look at the **West Edmonton Mall★** *(170th St. and 87th Ave., S of Trans-Canada 16. 403-444-5200 or 800-661-8890).* This vast and jostling complex of 800 department stores, restaurants, and specialty shops shares the same roof with a 25-ride amusement park, a full-size hockey rink, a beach with three-story water slides and *surf,* as well as a separate blue-water lake with a full-scale reconstruction of the *Santa Maria* and a flotilla of yellow submarines creeping across the bottom. And that's just for starters. There are alligators, penguins, fountains, bands, a miniature golf course, dolphins, and an adjoining 354-room fantasy-suite hotel. When you've had enough, run for one of 59 exits and try to find your car in one of the 20,000 spaces.

Deep Sea Adventure, West Edmonton Mall

Next, head south to **Fort Edmonton Park★★** *(Off the Whitemud Freeway. 403-496-8775. Mid-May–Labor Day, call for off-season hours; adm. fee),* a first-rate living history park depicting four periods from Edmonton's past. Ride a steam train down to the river, and walk through the vertical log walls of Fort Edmonton as it existed in 1846. A marvel of authentic reconstruction (pegged-log walls, deer-hide windowpanes, wrought-iron latches), this Hudson's Bay Company trading post and its costumed interpreters could easily consume an entire afternoon. Elsewhere, the park lays out the city's history along three streets of buildings, each representing a different phase in Edmonton's transition from farm town to city.

Downtown, tour the **Alberta Legislature Building** *(108th St. and 97th Ave. 403-427-7362. Closed Sat. Nov.-Feb.),* or trace the course of Canadian art at the **Edmonton Art Gallery** *(102nd Ave. at 99th St. 403-422-6223. Adm. fee).* To the west, the **Provincial Museum of Alberta★** *(12845 102nd Ave. 403-453-9100. Closed Mon. in winter; adm. fee)* folds a billion years of natural and human history into four galleries covering geology, wildlife, native peoples, and pioneers. But you'll find the most engaging exhibits in the **Live Insect Gallery★★,** giant cockroaches, scorpions and tarantulas, glistening centipedes, and white-eyed assassin bugs—most of them alive, even the death-feigning beetles.

Flying tern, Elk Island National Park

For a taste of how Edmonton's grandees lived at the turn of the century, cross the river to the university campus and tour **Rutherford House Provincial Historic Site** *(11153 Saskatchewan Dr. 403-427-3995. Adm. fee),* the restored Edwardian mansion of Alberta's first prime minister. Next, head back through town and smell the flowers at the **Muttart Conservatory** *(9626 96A St. 403-496-8755. Adm. fee),* a cluster of glass pyramids reproducing tropical, arid, and temperate climates.

For a break from the city, cruise through **Elk Island National Park★** *(E of Edmonton on Trans-Canada 16. 403-992-2950. Adm. fee),* a haven where two subspecies of bison roam. Compare the woolly forequarters and massive heads of the plains bison with their clean-cut relatives, the wood bison, then look for some of the park's harder-to-find wildlife: moose, elk, deer, and trumpeter swans.

East of the park, watch as settlers feed farm animals at the outstanding **Ukrainian Cultural Heritage Village★★** *(Off Trans-Canada 16. 403-662-3640. Mid-May–Oct.; adm. fee).* Learn how these hardworking, adaptable people broke free from hopeless peasants' lives in Eastern Europe and see how they lived once they got here—in grim sod-roofed huts and thatched houses, later in frame farmhouses or in town. Chat with the blacksmiths about the war in Europe (this is 1917, after all), or talk crops with the fellows at the general store. All the guides are exceptionally well versed.

Drive on to the **Basilian Fathers Museum★** *(5420 Sawchuk St., Mundare. 403-764-3887. Closed Sat.-Sun. Oct.-April; donation)* for a glimpse of Ukrainian spiritual life. Here you'll find books and manuscripts dating from the Middle Ages, a monastery, and a beautiful modern church.

Then, via Hwy. 2A, press on to **Wetaskiwin,** home of the **Reynolds-Alberta Museum**★★ *(Hwy. 13. 403-427-4321 or 800-661-4726. Closed Mon. Sept.-May; adm. fee),* an astounding collection of vintage autos, trucks, motorcycles, farm machinery, and aircraft, most restored to showroom condition. A gearhead's delight, the museum explores their development with videos, demonstrations, and other clever sideshows. In summer, putter around in vintage cars, or sputter overhead in an open-cockpit biplane *(weekends).*

On the western outskirts of **Red Deer** *(Visitor Center 403-346-0180),* learn about the 1885 Northwest Rebellion of Métis and native peoples at **Fort Normandeau Historic Site** *(32nd St. exit W off Hwy. 2. 403-346-2010. Mid-May–Labor Day; donation),* which includes a living history reconstruction of the fort, an interpretive center, and enticing picnic grounds on the Red Deer River. A pleasant riverside park system extends from the highway through town, taking in the **Kerry Wood Nature Centre and Gaetz Lakes Sanctuary** *(6300 45th Ave. 403-346-2010. Donation),* which examines the natural history of the Red Deer River Valley and the bird-busy pocket of woodlands, prairie meadows, swamps, and marshes.

For an ice-cream cone or a plate of pickled herring, take Rte. 592 west to ❺ **Markerville** and tour the **Historic Markerville Creamery** *(403-728-3006. Mid-May–Labor Day; adm. fee).* Once the heart of an Icelandic farm community, the creamery was the sole source of cash for turn-of-the-century farmers. One who pocketed cream checks here was Stephan G. Stephansson, considered one of the greatest poets writing in Icelandic since the Middle Ages. At **Stephansson House Provincial Historic Site** *(4 mi/7 km N of Markerville. 403-427-2022. Mid-May–Labor Day; adm. fee),* you can visit his simple home and tarry in his study, still furnished with his desk, daybed, and volumes of Icelandic literature.

Grain elevator, Ukrainian Cultural Heritage Village

Yoho to Kootenay

● 700 miles/1,125 km ● 6 to 7 days ● May through September

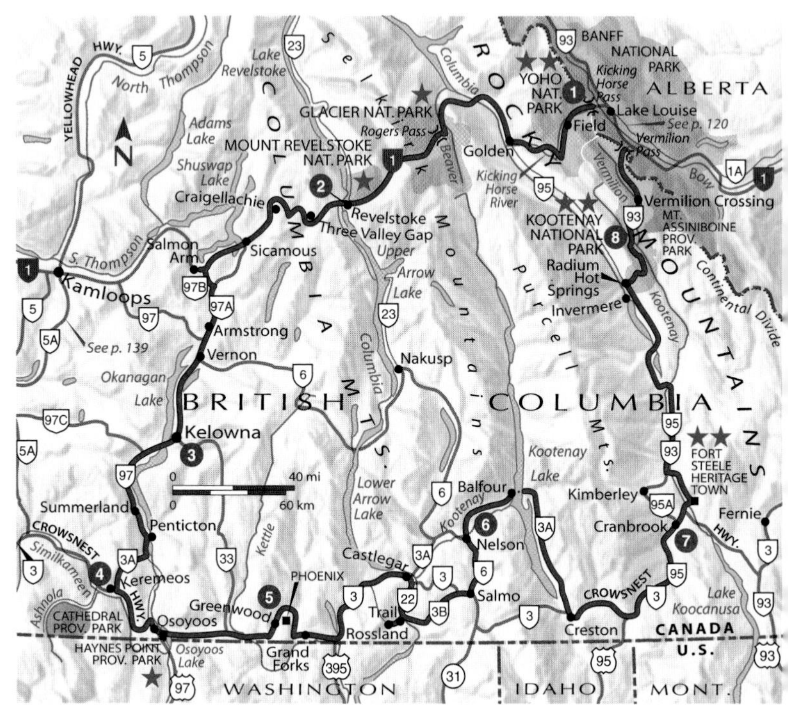

Starting on the crown of the continent, this route traces a wide circle through the mountains and valleys of southeastern British Columbia. Passing glaciers, alpine meadows, crashing rivers, inland lakes, and deep forests, it spins through a landscape of astonishing variety. The human story centers on railways and mining booms, sudden wealth and dashed hopes on a grand stage.

No name could be better than Yoho (a Cree word used to express awe) for the small but lavishly scenic ❶ **Yoho National Park★★** *(Visitor Center 250-343-6324. Adm. fee).* It starts on the Continental Divide where Trans-Canada 1 slices through the glacier-crested Bow Range before dropping steeply into the valley of the Kicking Horse River. You could do nothing more than drive that highway, stopping at viewpoints along the way, to feel amply rewarded. However, the real treasures of Yoho lie hidden in side valleys. One of the most famous is **Lake O'Hara★★,** whose scenic beauty cannot be overstated. All clichés apply: soaring mountains, turquoise waters, lush forest, and carpets of wildflowers. It's as if the mountains decided to create, in their most protected center, one perfect example of alpine landscaping. Wisely, park managers have restricted access—via a three-to-four-hour hike or limited shuttle service *(reservations required; fare)*. The superb 1920s **Lake O'Hara Lodge** *(250-343-6418, 403-678-4110 off season. June–mid-Oct. and Feb.–mid-April)* provides meals and accommodations. Once there, relax on the lakeshore, or walk a trail.

Back on the main road, stop at the **Lower Spiral Tunnel Viewpoint** to see where railroad engineers built two full-circle tunnels to reduce the dangerous 4.5 percent grade of the original Canadian Pacific Rail line (CPR). The view takes in a tunnel and the inviting **Yoho Valley,** squeezed between the mountains. Then take a side trip on Yoho Valley Road *(open mid-June–mid-Oct.; check for restrictions),*

Moon over Odaray Mountain near Lake O'Hara, Yoho National Park

and pause to view **Meeting-of-the-Waters,** the junction of the Kicking Horse and Yoho Rivers—the first one clear, the other laden with glacial silt. Drive past long scars left by avalanches that sweep down the wintry face of Wapta Mountain. In the valley, the waters of **Takakkaw Falls★** bleed from Daly Glacier and explode over a limestone cliff to become one of the highest waterfalls in Canada. From here, some of the park's best hiking trails climb into the alpine zone below the Wapta and Waputik Ice Fields.

Past **Field** (park headquarters and a division point for

the CPR), turn north to another beauty spot, **Emerald Lake★.** Along the way, check out **Natural Bridge,** where the river has tunneled its way through limestone. Emerald Lake glows green as if lit from within, a trick of glacial silt reflecting sunlight. If a good stiff hike sounds appealing, take the steep 3.4-mile trail to Hamilton Lake, in a lovely hanging valley on the slopes of Emerald Peak.

At Golden, the Rocky Mountains proper (characterized by layered sedimentary masses) are left behind. Ahead loom the lower Purcells and the higher Selkirks, part of the Columbia Mountains, older than the Rockies and composed of hard metamorphic rock. Enter Canada's **Glacier National Park★** *(250-837-7500. User fee includes Mount Revelstoke NP),* a high wilderness of ice, snow, and rock, stretched along the spine of the Selkirks. Primarily a hiker's park and a mountaineer's Shangri-la, it offers plenty to anyone willing to go slow and do a little walking.

Approaching **Rogers Pass,** notice the abandoned railroad bed on the slopes to the north. It seems an impossible place to run trains, yet engineers in the 1880s accomplished their work with snowsheds, enormous snowplows, and fierce determination, despite considerable loss of life. Nowadays, trains escape the worst hazards by using tunnels beneath the pass (highway traffic still takes the high route). Stop at the **Visitor Center★** *(250-837-6274. Call for hours)* for its excellent topographic models and tales of railroading in the barrel of an avalanche chute. A short trail leads along the original railbed.

West of the summit, the Illecillewaet and Asulkan Glaciers come into view dead ahead and high above. Turn in at the Illecillewaet campground road for day hikes into this spectacular high-alpine area. For a more protected experience, continue to the valley bottom and head into the peaceful shade of ancient giants at the wheelchair-accessible **Hemlock Grove Boardwalk.** Down the road, **Giant Cedars★** and **Skunk Cabbage** (wheelchair-accessible) provide short, rewarding, and easy entrées into the lush world of a temperate rain forest. These are both in **Mount Revelstoke National Park★** *(250-837-7500. User fee),* a relatively small park best known for the **Meadows in the Sky Parkway★** *(Closed in winter),* which climbs through forest to the gentle-but-scenic wildflower meadows of Mount Revelstoke.

In the 1860s, paddle-wheel steamers dropped gold

White Death

Rugged terrain made building a railroad over Rogers Pass a hard enough job, but keeping it open proved impossible. Avalanches carrying some of the heaviest snow accumulations in Canada repeatedly blocked the line. In 1899 an avalanche destroyed the station and roundhouse on the pass, killing eight. In another incident, men working to clear the tracks after one avalanche died when a second slide hit the same place. From 1885 to 1911, avalanche deaths totaled more than 200, and property damage was enormous. Admitting defeat, the Canadian Pacific Rail went underground by building the Connaught Tunnel.

seekers at the end of Upper Arrow Lake on land that would become the city of ❷ **Revelstoke.** From here, only rough bush trails continued north along the Columbia River. Gold fever ebbed, but railroad construction kept the town alive. Displays at the **Revelstoke Railway Museum**★ *(719 Track St. W. 250-837-6060. June-Sept., call for off-season hours; adm. fee)* tell of how the CPR was built and maintained, an epic story of geographic extremes, engineering feats, and strong-jawed determination. The museum's centerpiece is the great gleaming Locomotive No. 5468, an oil-powered steam engine that labored from 1948 to 1954.

Take in a musical revue or tour the ghost town down the road at **Three Valley Gap** *(250-837-2109. April–mid-Oct.; adm. fee).* Some buildings are reproductions, others were salvaged from area towns and reassembled on site.

Kids getting restless? Run off some steam on the shady trails of **The Enchanted Forest** *(Trans-Canada 1 between Revelstoke and Sicamous. 250-837-9477. Mid-May–mid-Sept.; adm. fee),* where storybook characters peek out from the foliage. If you like small things, head west to **Beardale Castle Miniatureland** *(250-836-2268. May-Sept.; adm. fee).*

Glacier National Park, British Columbia

Then test your skills with a genuine spike hammer at the **Craigellachie Last Spike Monument** *(Craigellachie. 250-836-3554. May-Sept.),* where the east and west lines of the CPR were joined on November 7, 1885.

Many-tentacled **Shuswap Lake** is a popular recreation area. Watch for western grebes at **Salmon Arm Nature Bay** *(Salmon Arm. 250-832-6247)*, one of the last large marsh areas to remain undeveloped in central British Columbia. The big show happens in May, when mating pairs of grebes get up and race across the bay as if water-skiing.

Leave Trans-Canada 1 near Salmon Arm and head south toward Vernon. Don't miss the turn to **Historic O'Keefe Ranch**★★ *(Hwy. 97. 250-542-7868. Mid-May–mid-Oct.; adm. fee)*, founded in 1867 and now a historic site. Pioneer rancher Cornelius O'Keefe recognized that, lucky or not, every miner needed to eat; transport companies needed livestock; bakers needed wheat; and builders needed wood. This meant prosperity for the ranch, which today stands as a symbol of how the region developed. His 1886 mansion is still graced with original furnishings, not at all reflecting the hard cowboy life. Close your eyes, listen to the lovely tones from the music box, and imagine what a haven this fine house must have represented.

Warm, dry Okanagan Valley is famous for fruit—and its wineries, many offering tours. In ❸ **Kelowna** the **B.C. Orchard Industry Museum**★ *(1304 Ellis St. 250-763-0433. July-Aug. Mon.-Sat., Sept.-June Tues.-Sat.; donation)* and **The Wine Museum** *(250-868-0441)* both preserve history along with the rich smells of the former packinghouse they occupy. The nearby **Kelowna Museum** *(470 Queensway Ave. 250-763-2417. July-Aug. Mon.-Sat., Sept.-June Tues.-Sat.; donation)* offers a surprising mix of items from around the world. At the south end of town, the **Father Pandosy Mission** *(Benvoulin Rd. 250-860-8369. April-Oct.; donation)* maintains buildings from an Oblate mission established circa 1860. A more elegant life is reflected at **Guisachan Heritage Park** *(1060 Cameron Ave. at Gorden Dr. 250-862-9368)*, the 1890s ranch home of the Earl and Countess of Aberdeen, now a historic site and restaurant.

Before highways were built, people and freight traveled on stern-wheelers like the **S.S. *Sicamous*** *(1099 Lakeshore Dr. W. 250-492-0403. Closed Sat.-Sun. in winter; adm. fee)*, in **Penticton.** From 1914 to 1936 its massive pitman arms, driven by huge pounding steam cylinders, must have been something to see, and hear. For more local history, visit the **R. N. Atkinson Museum** *(785 Main St. 250-490-2451. Closed Sun.; donation)*. What child (or adult) would pass up the chance to feed a giraffe? You can at the **Okanagan**

Time Travel

The living history program at **Fort Steele Heritage Town**★★ (see p. 137) lets you participate as much as you want. Tell a pompous politician what you think of his latest tax. Witness a crime, then testify at the frontier trial. Make old-fashioned ice cream, hear the ring of the blacksmith's anvil, or catch a horse-drawn wagon ride down Main Street.

B.C. Orchard Industry Museum, Kelowna

Game Farm *(5 mi/8 km S on Hwy. 97. 250-497-5405. Adm. fee).* Because their main business is stocking zoos and parks worldwide, the herds here are larger than in a zoo.

At the **Dominion Radio Astrophysical Observatory** *(White Lake Rd. off Hwy. 97, S of Penticton. 250-490-4355),* a large array of seven parabolic dishes catch radio waves that may be given off by interstellar gases. Exhibits explain how the radio images help reveal the composition of the universe.

From Penticton, Hwy. 3A cuts across to ❹ **Keremeos** and **The Grist Mill★** *(250-499-2888. Mid-May–mid-Oct., call for off-season hours; adm. fee),* an 1877 flour mill built to serve the gold traffic along the Dewdney Trail and recently restored to operating condition. Watch it work, then stroll through its heritage garden, a living plant museum. If you're looking for a picnic site, try the access road that parallels the lovely Ashnola River and surrounds **Cathedral Provincial Park** *(W of Keremeos. 250-494-6500. June-Sept.).*

Next, roll down the Similkameen Valley and over a low pass to the Okanagan Valley and **Osoyoos,** Canada's hot spot. You'll be told this is the northernmost extension of the Sonoran Desert—not ecologically true, but locals love the idea, and proudly tell of the day it hit 130°F in the shade—also doubtful. But it is a hot and curious place. **Haynes Point Provincial Park★** *(S of town, off Hwy. 97. 250-494-6500. April-Oct.)* occupies a narrow sand spit that reaches nearly across Osoyoos Lake. Look for such southern birds as California quail, canyon wrens, and white-throated swifts.

Dominion Radio Astrophysical Observatory

The depth and size of the Okanagan Valley becomes apparent as you climb out of it, heading east. Hwy. 3 generally follows the route of the Dewdney Trail, built in 1865 to provide a route through British territory for miners headed to the goldfields near Cranbrook. Pause to check out the fine old Victorians in ❺ **Greenwood** *(Board of Trade 250-445-6323),* whose turn-of-the-century prosperity was fueled by copper mining. Ask at the **Greenwood Museum** *(214 S. Copper St. 250-445-6355. May-Oct.; adm. fee)* about self-guided driving tours to mine sites and ghost towns, including **Phoenix,** built on a mountain of copper.

Around the turn of the century, **Castlegar** was the goal of Russian Doukhobors, pacifists and religious dissidents searching for cultural freedom under the slogan "Toil and Peaceful Life." Learn their story and visit a reconstructed communal settlement at **Doukhobor Historical Village★** *(Near airport. 250-365-6622. May-Sept.; adm. fee).* Next door, the **Kootenay Gallery of Art, History and Science** *(120 Heritage Way. 250-365-3337. Closed Mon. Sept.-June; donation)* shows traveling exhibits and work by regional artists.

Take a walk at **Zuckerberg Island Heritage Park** *(250-365-6440. Call for hours),* a city park at the junction of the Kootenay and Columbia Rivers, marked by the Russian Chapel House, an eccentric dwelling built by immigrant Alexander Zuckerberg. Interior Salishan people also wintered and fished on the island, as demonstrated by the full-scale model of a *kekuli,* or native pit house. For more local history, visit **The Castlegar & District Heritage Society** *(400 13th Ave. 250-365-6440. Donation).*

Doukhobor Historical Village, Castlegar

Shadowed by its vast lead-zinc smelter, **Trail** has based its economy on smelting for over a century. Ore used to arrive here from Rossland, where the **Rossland Historical Museum★★** *(Hwys. 22 and 3B. 250-362-7722. Mid-May–mid-Sept.; adm. fee)* offers tours of **Le Roi Mine,** now retired but once a world-famous producer of gold. Pick up a walking tour map for either city and visit sites spanning generations of mining and smelting. The smelter itself offers tours *(250-368-3144. Call for hours).*

From Salmo and beyond, Hwy. 6 punches a green furrow through the southern Selkirk Mountains, here rounded, clothed in conifer, and usually dripping with moisture. Emerge at ❻ **Nelson** *(Tourist info. 250-352-6033),* on the shore of enormous, fjordlike Kootenay Lake. For the most part, roads have replaced steamers as a means of transport, but a taste of the old days can be had by driving the lakeshore to Balfour, where a free ferry crosses to the lake's east side. At the lake's south end a series of marshes and wetlands have been set aside as **Creston Valley Wildlife Management Area★** *(Hwy. 3, W of Creston. 250-428-3260),* known for its tundra swans, wood ducks, ospreys, and Forster's terns. An interpretive center *(late April–mid-Oct.)* offers tours and information.

Creston Valley Wildlife Management Area

Hwy. 3 wanders pleasantly through orchards and forest to ❼ **Cranbrook** *(Chamber of Commerce 250-426-5914).* As divisional headquarters for the Crowsnest Branch of the CPR, the city has a long history of railroading. A work in progress, the **Canadian Museum of Rail Travel★** *(1 Van Horn St. 250-489-3918. Closed Sun.-Mon. Nov.-March; adm. fee)* will eventually display entire trains from different eras: The 1929 *Trans-Canada Limited* is already complete, to the point of serving lunch in the dining car. Others, like the 1907 *Soo-Spokane Train Deluxe,* are being restored.

Northeast, hard against the Rocky Mountains, is the site of a little-known but exceptionally rich 1864 Kootenay gold rush. One of the few remaining signs of that strike is **Fort Steele Heritage Town★★** *(Hwy. 93/95. 250-426-7352. Adm. fee for special summer programs).* Never actually a fort, it started as a ferry landing and grew to a supply town. It boomed again in 1897, when lead and silver were found nearby, but the whole shebang died in 1905 and stood empty for years. Today, more than 60 buildings, including many originals, interpret frontier life (see sidebar p. 134).

Heading north, Hwy. 93 parallels the grand western flank of the Rockies. At Radium Hot Springs, it slips through a crack in the wall into ❽ **Kootenay National Park★★** *(250-347-9505. May–mid-Sept.; adm. fee).* Just past the entrance station, stop for a soak at **Radium Hot Springs**

Pools★ *(250-347-9485 or 800-767-1611. Adm. fee),* then carry on through one of the Rockies' most dramatic gateways. From the narrow gap of Sinclair Canyon, the highway breaks out far above the gleaming Kootenay River. Typical of the Canadian Rockies, the mountains here are broad sedimentary masses shouldering through green forests to

Goodsir Peaks, on boundary between Yoho and Kootenay National Parks

alpine tundra and high snowfields. The park takes in two deep, classic glaciated valleys and the mountain slopes that give them shape. Pull over at the **Hector Gorge Viewpoint** for a look at the Vermilion River as it punches between the Mitchell and Vermilion ranges on its way to the Kootenay River. The rocky slopes of Mount Wardle, above the highway on the north, are favored by mountain goats. Watch for them close to the road, where the soil contains minerals that they crave. Ahead, past Wardle Creek, another mineral lick attracts more large animals including elk and moose.

Paint Pots Nature Trail leads a short distance to three cold mineral springs loaded with iron and surrounded by colorful oxidized clay once used for body paint, and later by Europeans for house paint. Don't miss **Marble Canyon★,** a slot cut deeply into the limestone and dolomite bedrock by Tokumm Creek. In places it is only a few yards across and some 197 feet deep, filled with tumbling water. Ahead lies **Vermilion Pass,** where in 1968 a forest fire burned 6,500 acres. The area is still recovering, as described in exhibits along a short self-guided trail at the pass. Ponder the ever renewing cycles of nature, and then continue on to Banff National Park (see p. 120).

Sea to Mountains★★

● **550 miles/885 km, plus ferry** ● **5 to 7 days** ● **May through September**

From western Canada's waterfront cities to the Coast Mountains' glacier-draped heights, this tour has a bit of everything—first-rate museums, strait crossings, and spectacular scenery mixed with history and the currents of strong and distinct cultures of the Northwest Coast tribes, the Far East, all parts of North America, and, of course, Britain.

The tour starts in Vancouver, hops a ferry to Victoria, skips along the coast of Vancouver Island and returns to the mainland for a sojourn among the glaciers at Whistler. It then scrambles through rough country inland along a gold rush trail to Kamloops, in the heart of cattle country. The route detours to the mighty Fraser River canyon before finally drifting back downriver to Vancouver.

Haida sculpture, Museum of Anthropology

❶ **Vancouver** *(Visitor Center 604-682-2222)* is a coastal city blessed by dramatic geography. Ocean water washes its shores, while close inland, mountains rise to snowcapped heights. First stop: the flower gardens of **Queen Elizabeth Park★** *(Cambie St. at 33rd St.)*. Right on top of the park, **Bloedel Conservatory★** *(604-257-8570. Adm. fee)* is a reminder that this is also a city of immigrants, many from across the Pacific. Beneath the glass dome, explore a wonderland of tropical songbirds, macaws, Japanese carp, Tasmanian tree ferns, Australian banyans, Moluccan cockatoos, and others.

Head west to S.W. Marine Drive, where the bewildering diversity at the **Botanical Garden** *(604-822-3928. Adm. fee)* will impress anyone from less favorable climates. Next travel on around the tip of Point Grey to the University of British Columbia and the **Museum of Anthropology** *(N.W. Marine Dr. 604-882-5087. Closed Mon. Labor Day–mid-May; adm. fee).* The main hall features the art of Northwest Coast First Nations peoples, who carved in grand scale: towering totem poles, oceangoing canoes, potlatch bowls with ladles up to 4 feet long, masks with moving parts, and bentwood storage boxes.

If you're feeling overwhelmed, walk across the road to **Nitobe Garden** *(604-822-9666. Adm. fee),* a classic walled Japanese garden designed to create a sense of visual harmony and emotional peace. It works. Then follow Fourth Avenue to the waterfront at Vanier Park, where the summer air is filled with kites, and sailboards dart among the yachts. Here the **Vancouver Museum★** *(604-736-4431. Tues.-Sun., under renovation, call for hours and exhibits; adm. fee)* features excellent rotating exhibits with a focus on the city's history. In the same building, the **H.R. MacMillan Planetarium** *(604-738-7827. Adm. fee)* presents a continuous schedule of multimedia shows.

Vancouver skyline, from Granville Island

Stroll along the shoreline to the **Vancouver Maritime Museum★** *(1905 Ogden Ave. 604-257-8300. Closed Mon. Sept.–mid-May; adm. fee),* whose centerpiece is the restored *St. Roch,* a Royal Canadian Mounted Police supply-and-patrol vessel built for the Arctic. It was the first ship to navigate the Northwest Passage from west to east, on a 27-month journey begun in 1942. Peer at the fine details of the ship model collection, then use the spotting scopes to view modern freighters in English Bay.

The city's crowning urban glory might well be its least urban feature—the green peninsula of **Stanley Park** with its winding drives, towering cedars, and footpaths. Allow several hours for the park and **Vancouver Aquarium★★** *(Stanley Park. 604-268-9900. Adm. fee),* a superb facility that celebrates marine life of the northwest. From here, take Hwy. 99 across the Lions Gate Bridge to North Vancouver and Capilano Canyon, where the **Grouse Mountain Skyride** *(604-984-0661. Fare)* climbs almost 3,000 vertical feet to a view of city and inlet. To stay closer to sea level, follow Marine Drive west to **Lighthouse Park.** Established in 1881 as a lighthouse reserve, it contains a remnant stand of old-growth Douglas-fir. Trails lead through the cathedral-like shadows of the ancient cedar and fir trees to the lighthouse on a rocky shoreline.

Even on hot summer days, Vancouver is blessed by near-constant ocean breezes. To get out in it, drive south on Hwy. 99 to the Tsawwassen Ferry Terminal *(604-669-1211),* and take passage to Victoria. Crossing the Strait of Georgia, you realize that for all its water, Vancouver is not an oceanfront city. It stands protected by numerous small islands (through which the ferry sails) and one very large one: Vancouver Island itself. An hour into the passage, a long chain of snowcapped peaks comes into view: the Olympic Mountains in Washington State. The white dome to the east is Mount Baker, also in Washington.

The ferry docks at Swartz Bay, and you make your entry to ❷ **Victoria** *(Visitor Center 604-953-2033)* by driving south on Hwy. 17 to the southeastern tip of Vancouver Island. The heart of the city is its inner harbor. When Captain Cook sailed up the coast in 1778, it was a wild place of dark forest and cold watery silence. A century later the trees had been replaced by a forest of masts—the sailing ships of Queen Victoria's empire.

Today the harbor is a delightful place to spend an afternoon. Begin on the waterfront promenade, among seagulls and artists and musicians. Stroll through the lobby of the grand **Empress Hotel** *(East side of the harbor. 604-384-8111)* recognized by its many steep-sloping green

Bentwood Boxes

The Northwest Coast tribes are famous for their cedar carvings. Among the more intriguing are bentwood boxes. A close look reveals that the sides are made from a single plank—scored, steamed, and folded. The corner where the two ends meet is pegged or sewn together with spruce roots and cedar withes. The closely fitted bottom is attached in the same way, creating a watertight storage container. Most have one-piece lids; many are carved and decorated with opercula shells and other native materials.

copper roofs. If you've dressed properly (no jeans), you can take afternoon tea and experience the British elegance so cherished here. Next door, **Miniature World** *(604-385-9731. Adm. fee)* is a modeler's heaven filled with tiny scenes from storybooks and history. Across the street, visit the **Royal British Columbia Museum★★** *(675 Belleville St. 604-387-3701. Adm. fee).* Walk through the history of settlement and immigration, or let the First Peoples' Gallery transport you back to the time of potlatches, giant canoes, and men dressed as eagles.

Inner harbor, Victoria

At night, outlined with tiny white lights, the weathered copper domes and heavily ornamented facade of the **British Columbia Legislative Building★** *(604-387-3046. Closed Sat.-Sun. Labor Day–May)* takes on a festive air that belies the heavy politics carried out inside. Opposite, the **Royal London Wax Museum★** *(470 Belleville St. 604-388-4461. Adm. fee)* offers the usual figures of British royalty along with other celebrities, Disney characters, and a very realistic chamber of horrors (inspect it before letting the kids enter). The neighboring **Undersea Gardens** *(604-382-5717. Adm. fee)* is a floating aquarium with the added attraction of divers who bring critters like wolf eels to the window.

Check out the impressive grouping of tiny craft in the Solo Circumnavigation Gallery of the **Maritime Museum of British Columbia★** *(28 Bastion Square. 604-385-4222. Adm. fee).* There are some 400 ship models and the *Trekka,* a 20-foot yawl that sailed around the world in 1955. It seems impossibly frail, even in this protected setting. Other galleries feature the voyages of Capt. James Cook and models of the Canadian Pacific steam liners. The museum occupies the former Provincial Law Courts Building, only one of many old redbrick structures in the historic district.

View a rich collection of Japanese art at the **Art Gallery of Greater Victoria★** *(1040 Moss St. 604-384-4101.*

Adm. fee), then climb the tower of **Craigdarroch Castle★** *(1050 Joan Crescent. 604-592-5323. Adm. fee),* a five-story residence built by coal baron Robert Dunsmuir in 1890. Visitors can enjoy its lavish interior, which is more than Dunsmuir ever did. He died before it was finished.

Butchart Gardens, Victoria

You could happily spend all your time in the heart of Victoria, but a few excursions are worthwhile. First choice is **Butchart Gardens★★** *(800 Benvenuto Ave., off Hwy. 17A. 604-652-4422. Adm. fee).* This is not a place to visit in a hurry; allow time for the intoxicating effects of color and natural fragrance. Begun near the turn of the century with Jennie Butchart's efforts to soften the appearance of the family cement factory and limestone quarry, it grew into one of the island's chief beauty spots. The Sunken Garden is a particular wonder, considering that its rolling waves of blossoms occupy the old quarry itself, once a scene of shattered stone.

If you have an interest in the times before Queen Victoria, visit **Anne Hathaway's Thatched Cottage★** *(429 Lampson St. 604-388-4353. Adm. fee),* a full-size reproduction of the 16th-century house of Shakespeare's wife. Guides in period costume delight in describing the origin of many English expressions while touring the 16th- and 17th-century furnishings. From here it's not far to **Fort Rodd Hill** and **Fisgard Lighthouse National Historic Site** *(603 Fort Rodd Hill Rd. 604-478-5849. Adm. fee).* The coastal gun batteries, built to protect an imperial coaling station, never saw action, but the lighthouse (oldest on Canada's west coast) has been an important beacon since 1860.

Fragrant water lilies, Butchart Gardens

Tear yourself away from Victoria, and follow Trans-Canada 1 as it rolls north toward the ferry dock in Nanaimo. Along the way, ride a steam train and hear the story of what is still the province's largest industry at the **B.C. Forest Museum** *(2892 Drinkwater Rd., Chemainus. 250-715-1113. Mid-April–mid-Oct.; adm. fee).*

❸ **Nanaimo** offers a few reasons to take a later ferry. Explore the rocks and coves of **Newcastle Island Provincial Marine Park** *(By passenger ferry. 604-387-4363),* or visit

The Bastion *(Front St.),* a wooden gun tower built in 1853 to protect the harbor. Then learn about the coal mines that earned Robert Dunsmuir of Craigdarroch Castle all that money. The coal story, among others, is outlined at the **Nanaimo District Museum** *(100 Cameron Rd. 604-753-1821. Closed Sun.-Mon. Labor Day–late May; adm. fee).*

It would be nice at this point to stay longer—to drive north along the coast, go on a whale-watching trip, visit Strathcona Provincial Park—but our route heads to the ferry dock *(604-753-6626)* and back to the mainland for an excursion among glaciers.

Disembark at Horseshoe Bay, turn north and follow the coast road along spectacular **Howe Sound,** one of British Columbia's trademark fjords. The glaciers that

Fisgard Lighthouse National Historic Site, Victoria

carved this narrow channel also smoothed the rocks on both sides, exposing valuable ore near Britannia. The copper mine here once employed 60,000 people and turned out over 50 million tons of concentrate. Now it houses the **B.C. Museum of Mining** *(Britannia Beach. 604-688-8735. Museum open May-Oct., interpretive center also open Nov.-April Mon.-Fri.; adm. fee).*

A few miles farther, at ❹ **Shannon Falls Provincial Park★** *(604-898-3678),* walk the short trail to British Columbia's third highest waterfall (1,100 feet). The look-out point is set among tall cedar and fir, which seem big enough except for the huge stumps that tell of even greater giants that once grew here.

Past Squamish, rock climbers appear like spiders on the monolith of granite called **Stawamus Chief.** From here, the road begins a long climb toward the mountain and ski resort of **Whistler★★** *(Resort Association 604-932-3928),* also a full summer destination with restaurants, golf courses, river-running, hiking, and all the rest. The highspot, literally, is a chairlift ride to the top of Blackcomb Mountain. Rising through forest and meadow, you step off on a rocky ridge a full mile above the valley floor. At your feet, Horstman Glacier is crowded with skiers even on the warmest day. **Garibaldi Provincial Park** *(604-898-3678),* a wilderness of glacier-clad peaks, stretches into the distance. Trails lead in that direction, and also back down the mountain; you can choose to walk part way, as suits the weather and your mood.

Lillooet District Museum

Leaving Whistler, the highway drops scenically toward Pemberton. If your legs are not too stiff from hiking, take the trail at **Nairn Falls Provincial Park** to where the Green River's glacial waters explode through a narrow canyon. The road lingers in the relative openness of the Pemberton Valley, then begins an ear-popping climb to Duffey Lake Pass. At **Joffre Lakes Provincial Recreation Area★,** take a five-minute walk through the cool forest to Lower Joffre Lake and thundering views of the Matier Glacier and surrounding peaks. Then it's down and down as the road plummets to the valley of the Fraser River.

5 **Lillooet,** which occupies flat benches above the river, got its start in the 1858 gold rush, and within two years mushroomed into a typically rowdy frontier supply town. Having struggled inland on the Harrison Trail, prospectors paused here to gather courage for the onward push to the goldfields at Barkerville in the Cariboo Mountains.

For a short time, Lillooet marked Mile Zero of the Cariboo Wagon Road, commemorated now by a cairn on Main Street. In later years, the town gained some fame from Ma Murray, plain-spoken publisher of the *Bridge River-Lillooet News* (see sidebar this page). The contents of Murray's office, presses and all, occupy the basement of the **Lillooet District Museum★** *(790 Main St. 604-256-4308. May-Nov.; donation).* Ask for a history map giving directions to gold rush landmarks like the old hanging tree on the hill above town, and the neatly piled river cobbles left by Chinese miners who made profits by re-processing the placer claims of less thorough miners.

Lillooet News

When he ran for the B.C. Legislative Assembly, George Murray promised voters a newspaper. He gave them that, and his wife as editor, in 1934. Ma Murray soon became famous for her down-to-earth, irreverent editorials. Her masthead read: "Printed in the sagebrush country of the Lillooet every Thursday, God willing. Guarantees a chuckle every week and a belly laugh once a month or your money back. Subscriptions $6 in Canada. Furiners $8. Circulation 1,573 this week and every bloody one paid for."

Hwy. 99 crosses the mighty Fraser, then rolls through dry grassy hills to the Thompson River Valley. This is Canada's dry belt, the parched interior, where summer temperatures rise above 100 degrees, and the sun would send a Texas lizard looking for shade. About 7 miles (11 km) north of Cache Creek, **Historic Hat Creek Ranch★** *(604-457-9722 or 800-782-0922. Mid-May–mid-Oct.; adm. fee)* was once a roadhouse and supply point on the Cariboo Wagon Road. Hop on the restored stagecoach for a ride around the grounds, which include a traditional Shuswap native winter home and the original log cabin that grew into a two-story rambling and ramshackle hotel.

Continue east through brown hills, ponderosa pine, and occasional prickly pear cactus to **Kamloops.** You can learn about area history at the **Kamloops Museum and Archives★** *(207 Seymour St. 604-828-3576. Donation),* where exhibits describe the city's first days as a Hudson's Bay Company post, and follow events through the gold rush to more recent times. For a glimpse of First Nations' culture, go north across town to **Secwepemc Museum and Native Heritage Park★** *(335 Yellowhead Hwy. 604-828-9801. Closed Sat.-Sun. Labor Day–May; adm. fee).* View the artifacts, then step outside to an archaeological site and a reconstructed village. If the high country is on your mind, head for the ski lifts and alpine flower meadows of **Sun Peaks Resort** *(N on Hwy. 5 to Heffley Creek, then E on Tod Mountain Rd. 604-578-7842).*

Leaving Kamloops, Hwy. 5A climbs south over the gentle hills of what settlers called the Empire of Grass. This is cattle country, where huge ranches were established starting in the 1870s. Stop in for a drink or a meal at the 1908 **Quilchena Hotel★** *(Quilchena. 604-378-2611. May–mid-Oct.),* and ask about the bullet holes in the bar.

At Merritt, Hwy. 5A joins the Coquihalla Hwy., the four-lane toll road to the coast. **Coquihalla Canyon** is the shortest route from Vancouver to the interior, but it's never been easy. In 1916 the Kettle Valley Railway was forced through with great difficulty and expense. Going the 54 miles from Hope to Brookmere required 13 tunnels, 15 snowsheds, and 54 bridges. At ❻ **Coquihalla Canyon Provincial Recreation Area★,** walk the abandoned railbed to a series of four tunnels above the river.

If time allows, drive up the canyon and ride the **Hell's Gate Airtram★★** *(Trans-Canada 1 near Boston Bar. 604-*

Taming the Rush

From Hope, a side trip up the Fraser River visits important gold rush sites. British authorities tried to avoid the mayhem of American mining booms, but no force could stem the wild excitement brought on by the prospect of sudden wealth. The two seeming opposites stand side by side in **Yale:** The **Historic Yale Museum★** *(604-863-2324. Daily July-Aug., Sat.-Sun. April and Oct., Thurs.-Mon. June and Sept.; adm. fee)* tells the mining story, while the Anglican **Church of St. John the Divine★,** built in 1860 and fully restored, represents the higher powers of God and king.

867-9279. April-Oct.; fare) over the gorge to the edge of boiling rapids in the 110-foot-wide canyon. A footbridge offers a white-knuckled view directly above the waters. Don't miss the salmon exhibit, which tells how a system of fishways reopened the river after railroad construction debris virtually ended the ancient cycle of their migrations. Just downstream, **Alexandra Bridge Provincial Park** offers picnic sites and views of the river from an old suspension bridge. From here, it's back down the Fraser River Valley to Vancouver, a couple of hours by car if you go straight.

Fraser Canyon, north of Yale

Instead, stay northwest of the river and follow Hwy. 7 to Hot Springs Road and **Harrison Hot Springs Hotel** *(604-796-2244),* a lakeside resort with outdoor and indoor mineral soaks. The steamy water would feel good on a cold day, but in summer the woodland lakes of neighboring **Sasquatch Provincial Park** are more appealing. No Bigfoot visible here, except on advertising signs in town.

Now cross the Fraser and take Trans-Canada 1 to Langley and **Fort Langley National Historic Site**★ *(Mavis St. 604-888-4424. Adm. fee).* Formerly a distribution point for the Hudson's Bay Company, the fort is now a living history museum set up to re-create conditions in the 1850s. Talk hoops with a cooper (barrelmaker) or try to convince the head clerk that B.C. will some day be part of an independent nation called Canada. Fat chance.

As a last stop before Vancouver, consider **New Westminster,** once the capital of the Crown Colony of British Columbia. Head for the waterfront and step aboard the **S.S. *Samson V* Maritime Museum** *(604-522-6894. Call for hours; donation).* Last of the stern-wheel snag boats and deadhead grubbers, the *Samson V* worked to keep the Fraser River free of obstructions from 1937 to 1980, when it retired in working condition.

Gold Country★

● 525 miles/845 km ● 5 to 6 days ● Mid-to-late summer ● Plan your trip around the ferry schedule between Haines and Skagway (Alaska Marine Hwy. System: 907-465-3941 or 800-642-0066. Fare). Ferries book up long in advance, do not run every day, and often depart at inconvenient times.

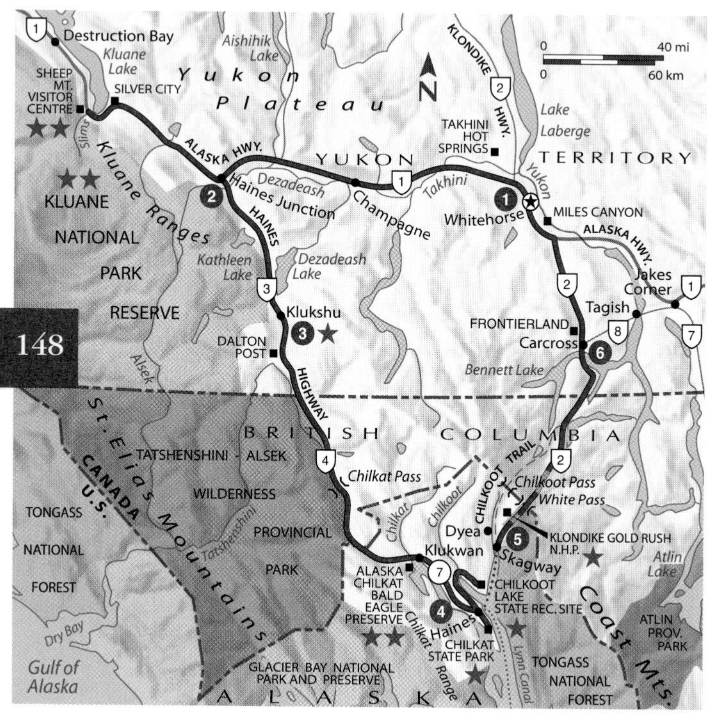

Enriched by two major First Nations cultures and enlivened by the history of the Klondike gold rush, this gloriously scenic drive through the Yukon's southwest corner takes in a tremendous variety of landscapes, and offers abundant opportunities for spotting wildlife—especially grizzly bears and bald eagles. Enroute, it cruises through the broad rolling forests of the Yukon interior, skirts Kluane National Park Reserve's wall of glacier-gouged peaks, climbs above tree line, then plunges through dense coastal forest to magnificent fjords. There are also stops to watch the inland Tutchone people fish for salmon, to visit coastal Tlingit wood-carvers, and to learn about the grueling rush to the Klondike goldfields in 1897.

The trip begins in ❶ **Whitehorse** *(Chamber of Commerce 403-667-7545),* capital of the Yukon Territory and an important gold rush landmark. It sprang to life as a transportation hub between the goldfields near Dawson City, 36 hours north by steamboat, and the port of Skagway, 110 miles south by rail.

Downtown, along the startling blue waters of the Yukon River, step onto the stitched-canvas decks of a beached but gleaming 1930s paddle wheeler at the **S.S. *Klondike* National Historic Site★★** *(403-667-3910. Mid-May–mid-Sept.; adm. fee)*. Spirited guides, well versed in riverboat lore, lead the way through the vast cargo deck to the engine room, cabins, crew quarters, and wheelhouse.

A short stroll downriver takes you to the **MacBride Museum** *(1st Ave. and Wood St. 403-667-2709. Mid-May–Labor Day; adm. fee),* where you can peer into a tiny log cabin that once belonged to Sam McGee, the heat-craving subject of the famous Robert Service ballad. Other exhibits sketch the natural and cultural history of the Yukon.

Next, drop by the **Yukon Transportation Museum★** *(By the airport. 403-668-4792. Mid-May–Labor Day; adm. fee),* where a moose-skin boat, a dog sled, railroad cars, sleighs, a ski-plane, and old photos act as a time line of the region's history. Something in these frail and battered artifacts conveys a haunting sense of the Yukon's ferocious climate, its daunting terrain, and the adventurous spirit of its people. Nearby, have a look at what locals tout as the **World's Largest Weathervane**—a Douglas DC-3 mounted high on a pedestal.

A few miles south the Yukon River flows through **Miles Canyon,** a narrow gorge walled by low, nearly vertical basalt cliffs. During the gold rush, this canyon and its once turbulent waters formed a major obstacle, soon bypassed by a log-rail tramline drawn by horses. A tent town, **Canyon City,** boomed at the head of the bottleneck. Both disappeared when the railroad opened in 1900. In summer, guided hikes *(Yukon Conservation Society 403-668-5678)* depart twice daily from the footbridge spanning the river.

Wheelhouse on S.S. *Klondike,* Whitehorse

Heading west from Whitehorse, the Alaska Hwy. glides over the southern fringe of the Yukon Plateau, a vast, rumpled landscape where the mountains stand as dark,

Kathleen Lake, Kluane National Park Reserve

rounded humps separated by spacious woodland valleys. As the Takhini River Valley opens up, you'll notice a different sort of mountain range to the south, higher, sharper, and more serrated: the Coast Mountains.

For thousands of years, this region has been home to the Southern Tutchone people—Athapaskan who fished, hunted, trapped, and traded without direct contact with Europeans until the mid-19th century. For an enlightening glimpse into their life, stop at the **Long Ago People's Place**★ *(Just E of Champagne. 403-667-6375. Tours May-Oct.; adm. fee),* where the old ways are studied, practiced, and revered. Duck into a winter shelter made of moose and caribou skins, and learn how the Tutchone tanned hides, dried fish, and hunted with ingenious traps and tools.

From Champagne, the road picks up the Dezadeash River and heads toward the jaw-dropping ramparts of the Kluane Ranges. This abrupt line of massive, deeply glaciated peaks stands above a sprawling forested valley, dwarfs the tiny crossroads town of ❷ **Haines Junction,** and extends along the entire eastern front of **Kluane National Park Reserve**★★ *(403-634-7250).* Beyond this imposing wall lies the heart of the park—a vast, forbidding, and intensely wild landscape where the world's largest nonpolar ice fields nearly bury Canada's highest peaks, the St. Elias Mountains.

Though relatively few glaciers are visible from the road, roughly 2,000 of them cover nearly three-quarters of the park's 8,500 square miles. Often reaching depths of a mile or more, they go beyond the park's western border into

Bush Pilot Blowpots

The Yukon's early bush pilots, who displayed a cheerful indifference to harrowing flights, faced another hazard just to keep their planes operational in winter. Due to the extreme night cold, a pilot had to drain the oil from the plane's engine, keeping it warm overnight or reheating it in the morning before replacing it. But first, the pilot had to warm the engine by placing a "blowpot" underneath the plane's nose, which was draped in tarp to block wind—an arrangement that led to fires for the unlucky flyboy.

the Gulf of Alaska and cling to the upper reaches of Canada's highest summit, 19,545-foot Mount Logan. For most travelers, this isolated realm remains hidden behind the verdant and compelling Kluane Ranges, which form a corridor of priceless habitat for bears, Dall's sheep, mountain goats, moose, wolves, and 118 species of birds.

Get a handle on the park at the Visitor Reception Centre *(Haines Junction. 403-634-7250. May-Sept.; fee for guided hikes),* where modest exhibits summarize Kluane's natural history. Consider taking an interpretive hike, or hiring a private outfitter for horseback rides, raft trips, or flights over the ice fields. Then follow the Alaska Hwy. northwest along the mountains to the Yukon's largest lake, **Kluane Lake,** which stretches 40 miles beneath a row of high, glaciated peaks. If ghost towns interest you, take the turnoff for **Silver City**, built during a short-lived 1904 gold rush.

Farther north, cross the mudflats of the Slims River Delta and pull into the **Sheep Mountain Visitor Centre★★** *(Mid-May–mid-Sept.)* to learn about Dall's sheep, Kluane's most abundant large mammal. Beginning in late August, these white relatives of the Rocky Mountain bighorn sheep gather in great numbers on the slopes.

Dall's sheep

Return to Haines Junction and follow the Haines Hwy. south. Stop and stretch your legs along the forested shore of **Kathleen Lake,** where rock and gravel peaks burst 5,000 feet from the water, or scramble up **Rock Glacier Trail,** which traverses a pile of rubble left by a glacier and offers a fine view of Dezadeash Lake.

During the summer and autumn spawning runs of king, sockeye, and coho salmon, you can watch the Southern Tutchone use traditional methods to trap, butcher, and dry fish at ❸ **Klukshu★** *(403-634-2288. Mid-May–mid-Sept.; photos by permission only),* a small village of log cabins that may be the oldest settlement in the Yukon. Farther south, as many as 300 Tutchone gather at **Dalton Post**

(52 mi/84 km S of Haines Junction, via steep, unmarked gravel road) to catch salmon with gaff hooks attached to long poles. A native settlement long before Jack Dalton established a trading post here during the 1890s, the site is now abandoned most of the year. Watch for bears.

Soon the highway climbs into British Columbia, emerges from the trees, and stretches off. At the **Chilkat Pass,** bid farewell to the high country for now and begin the nearly 4,000-foot plunge to Haines, Alaska. This spectacular stretch of road swings past jagged mountain crests draped with glaciers and plummets through forest to the broad, gravelly floor of the Chilkat River Valley. In late fall, roughly 4,000 American bald eagles—the world's greatest concentration—gather along the silty Chilkat to roost in the cottonwoods and waddle about the alluvial flats, picking at salmon. The **Alaska Chilkat Bald Eagle Preserve★★** *(Alaska State Parks 907-766-2292)* protects 48,000 acres of river bottomlands to keep the birds coming back.

Overlooking a stunning fjord gripped by 6,000-foot peaks, ❹ **Haines** *(Visitor Center 907-766-2234 or 800-458-3579)* is a small port and tourist town. On a grassy slope above the harbor stand the tidy white clapboard buildings of **Fort William H. Seward National Historic Landmark.** An active military base from 1903 through World War II, its buildings are now private residences, inns, and shops. A replica of a Tlingit clan house stands on the parade grounds. Nearby, native dancers interpret ancient Tlingit legends at the **Chilkat Center for the Arts★** *(13 Fort Seward Dr. 907-766-2160. Call for performance times; adm. fee).* Downtown, the **Sheldon Museum and Cultural Center★** *(Main and Front Sts. 907-766-2366. Closed Sat. Oct.–mid-May; adm. fee)* summarizes pioneer history, but its real strength lies in interpreting Tlingit culture through artifacts such as blankets, wood carvings, body armor, bentwood boxes, and a large dugout canoe.

Drying salmon, Klukshu

Southeast of Haines, **Chilkat State Park★** *(Alaska State Parks 907-465-4563)* sits on a steep finger of land offering seaside and mountain hikes with dazzling views. For a chance to see grizzly bears snagging salmon during spawn-

Salmon counting, Dalton Post

ing runs, follow the ferry road around the point and up the Chilkoot River to **Chilkoot Lake State Recreation Site★.** The view makes the drive worthwhile, wildlife or not.

From Haines, board the **Alaska Marine Highway** *(907-465-3941 or 800-642-0066. Fare)* ferry and look for whales as your ship glides across the water and heads up the narrow Taiya Inlet to ❺ **Skagway** *(Visitor Center 907-983-2855).* Once a major gateway for the Klondike gold rush and now a tourist town, Skagway lies at the mouth of a slender canyon crowded by high stony peaks. In two years, some 30,000 prospectors paused here or at nearby Dyea before setting off on one of two grueling routes over Alaska's Coast Ranges: White Pass and Chilkoot Pass. Both were old Tlingit trade routes, converging 35 miles north at Bennett Lake, where the stampeders built or bought boats for the 500-mile river journey to Dawson City.

A lawless place early on, Skagway settled down with the completion in 1900 of the White Pass & Yukon Route Railroad, which hauled supplies north to Whitehorse and returned with gold dust and, later, silver ore. The tracks also soon attracted well-heeled tourists in cruise ships.

Brush up on gold rush history at the restored 1898 train depot, now a Visitor Center for the **Klondike Gold Rush National Historical Park★** *(2nd Ave. and Broadway. 907-983-2921).* A film tracks the stampede north from Seattle to Dawson City, and weathered artifacts and exhibits concentrate on the rigors of the various routes to the goldfields. A ranger walk through the historic district orients visitors to Skagway's old buildings and gold rush characters.

Nearby, climb aboard the **White Pass & Yukon Route**

Grease Trails

The grueling trails that pressed Klondike stampeders to the limit had been used for generations by Tlingit trading with the Tutchone and other interior native peoples. Dubbed "Grease Trails" because the Tlingit stock in trade was a valuable oil rendered from smelt, the routes were jealously guarded well into the 19th century, with the Tlingit eventually acting as middlemen between Europeans, who wanted furs, and the interior peoples, who wanted Europe's manufactured goods.

Railroad★★ *(Depot, 2nd Ave. and Broadway. 907-983-2217 or 800-343-7373. Mid-May–mid-Sept.; fare)* and follow in the footsteps of the sourdoughs from the swaying comfort of a vintage parlor car. The narrow-gauge trains climb through the tortuous Skagway River gorge, traversing sheer cliffs and barreling through tunnels before breaking out onto the broad alpine meadows of White Pass. Round trip: three hours. The same journey took months during the rush, when each man made many trips over the 40-mile trail in order to pack his year's worth of supplies to the Canadian border.

Locomotive, White Pass & Yukon Route Railroad

Back in town, visit the **Trail of '98 Museum** *(907-983-2420. Mid-May–mid-Sept.; adm. fee),* a collection of mostly pioneer artifacts housed in the striking 1899 **Arctic Brotherhood Hall,** which resembles a giant basket, thanks to the thousands of pieces of driftwood nailed to its facade.

Out at the **Gold Rush Cemetery** *(Just N of town),* the humble grave of Skagway's preeminent villain, Soapy Smith, lies within spitting distance of a granite monument erected by the grateful town to Frank Reid, the man who shot Soapy and then died from wounds sustained in their gunfight. Nearby, **Reid Falls** dodges down a shrubby chasm.

Little remains of **Dyea** *(Pick up map in Skagway),* once a

Along Haines Hwy. near Dalton Post

town of 8,000 and jump-off point for the **Chilkoot Trail.** Hardy backpackers still hike the Chilkoot *(permit required on Canada side),* now festooned with rusty tin cans, bed-springs, horse bones, and other artifacts of gold rush days. For a more relaxed jaunt, follow a ranger through the Sitka spruce forest, dune grasses, and fireweed that mask the townsite *(contact Klondike Gold Rush N.H.P. 907-983-2921).*

Returning to Whitehorse, the road climbs the steep valley walls, roughly paralleling the old White Pass Trail. Roadside plaques identify historic points. Soon, you climb out of the gorge and top 3,292-foot **White Pass,** overlooking a broad, glaciated saddle of granite sparsely covered by tundra. Narrow **Summit Lake** winds alongside the highway for miles, eventually draining into the Yukon River.

From White Pass, descend into the gentler landscape of this part of the Yukon interior, with its immense lakes—including **Bennett Lake,** where 30,000 prospectors waited out the winter of 1898. The history is explored at the Visitor Center *(403-821-4431. Late May–late Sept.)* in ❻ **Carcross.** Across the street, browse at the **Matthew Watson General Store** *(403-821-3501. Mid-May–late Sept.),* the Yukon's oldest, then drive north to **Frontierland** *(403-667-1055. May-Sept.; adm. fee),* a cluster of frontier dwellings and home of the world's largest taxidermic polar bear.

Return to Whitehorse via Hwy. 2.

For More Information

NATIONAL PARKS & HISTORIC SITES
Web site for Canadian Heritage and Parks Canada: http://www.pch.gc.ca
Atlantic Region *506-328-1356* or *800-213-7275*
Quebec Region *418-648-4177* or *800-463-6769*
Ontario Region *416-954-9243* or *800-839-8221*
Prairie and Northwest Territories Region *204-983-2290* or *800-250-4567*
Alberta Region *800-748-7275*
Pacific and Yukon Region *604-666-0176*

TOURISM OFFICES
Travel Alberta *403-427-4321* or *800-661-8888*
Tourism British Columbia *604-663-6000* or *800-663-6000*
Travel Manitoba *204-945-3777* or *800-665-0040*
Tourism New Brunswick *800-561-0123*
Tourism Newfoundland and Labrador *709-729-2830* or *800-563-6353*
Northwest Territories Tourism *403-873-7200* or *800-661-0788*
Nunavut Tourism (The Northwest Territories will split in 1999, and the eastern portion will become the province of Nunavut) *819-979-6551* or *800-491-7910*
Nova Scotia Information and Reservations *902-424-5781* or *800-341-6096*
Ontario Travel *416-314-0944* or *800-668-2746*
Prince Edward Island Tourism *800-565-0267*
Tourisme Québec *514-873-2015* or *800-363-7777*
Tourism Saskatchewan *306-787-2300* or *800-667-7191*
Tourism Yukon *403-667-5340*

HOTEL & MOTEL CHAINS
Best Western International *800-528-1234*
Canadian Pacific Hotels 800-441-1414
Clarion Hotels *800-252-7466*
Comfort Inns *800-668-4200*
Days Inn *800-325-2525*
Embassy Suites *800-362-2779*
Hilton Hotels *800-HILTONS*
Holiday Inns *800-HOLIDAY*
Howard Johnson International *800-446-4656*
Quality Inns-Hotels-Suites *800-228-5151*
Radisson Hotels International *800-333-3333*
Ramada Inns *800-272-6232*
Rodeway Inn *800-228-2000*
Sheraton Hotels and Inns *800-325-3535*
Travelodge International, Inc. *800-578-7878*
Westin Hotels and Resorts *800-228-3000*

ILLUSTRATIONS CREDITS
Pierre St. Jacques photographed the Atlantic, Quebec, and Ontario chapters, except for the following pages: 19 Sam Abell, National Geographic Photographer; 25 John Eastcott/Yva Momatiuk; 26 Robert Madden, National Geographic Society; and 43 Alain Masson.

Michael Lewis photographed the Prairie and West chapters, except for the following pages: 102 George F. Mobley; 116 Sarah Leen; 117 Michael S. Yamashita; 126 Raymond Gehman; 131 Raymond Gehman; 133 George F. Mobley; 138 James D. Balog; 139 Ann E. Yow; and 151 Tom Bean.

ACKNOWLEDGMENTS
The Book Division wishes to thank the Canadian national and provincial governments for their assistance in preparing this book, especially Saverio Mancina; Tourism Section, Canadian Embassy, Washington, D.C.; Canadian Tourism Commission; and Canadian Heritage and Parks Canada.

NOTES ON AUTHORS AND PHOTOGRAPHERS
KATHERINE ASHENBURG, who wrote the Ontario chapter of the guide, is the author of *Going to Town: Architectural Walking Tours in Southern Ontario*. An editor at the *Globe and Mail* newspaper in Toronto, she wrote her Ph.D. thesis on Charles Dickens and is a regular contributor to the *New York Times* travel section.

Seasoned roadster and confirmed Canadophile, ALISON KAHN spent three years in Newfoundland. Her book, *Listen While I Tell You,* relates the story of the island's Jewish community. After completing her fieldwork, she wrote the guide's Atlantic and Quebec chapters at home in Maryland.

JEREMY SCHMIDT, author of the Saskatchewan and British Columbia chapters, writes for a number of international magazines, including National Geographic TRAVELER, *GEO,* and *Equinox*. He first traveled through the western United States and Canada as a 17-year-old hitchhiker, and 30 years later still enjoys wandering the cities and back roads. He lives in Jackson Hole, Wyoming.

THOMAS SCHMIDT has written extensively about the nature and history of the Rocky Mountain region, including *The Rockies,* the first book in this driving guide series. For *Canada,* he continued his travels to the mountains, in Alberta and the Yukon, as well as to the prairies of Manitoba. Tom lives in the Idaho foothills of the Tetons with his wife, Terese, and children, Patrick and Colleen.

MICHAEL LEWIS photographed Canada's western provinces for the guide. Other work includes magazine assignments and a book on Colorado's oldest farm and ranch families. He photographed the Rocky Mountain region for the first in this series of driving guides. Lewis lives in Denver with his wife, Sharon, and dogs, Carlos and Lucy.

This assignment was Canadian photographer PIERRE ST. JACQUES' first for the National Geographic Society. His 18 years of experience have taken him from bat caves to corporate boardrooms. He currently resides in the countryside outside Ottawa and enjoys travel and time with his two sons. He photographed the Ontario, Quebec, and Atlantic chapters of the guide.

Index

Index

Index

Composition for this book by the National Geographic Society Book Division. Printed and bound by R.R. Donnelly & Sons, Willard, Ohio. Color separations by Digital Color Image, Pensauken, New Jersey. Paper by Consolidated/Alling & Cory, WillowGrove, Pennsylvania. Cover printed by Miken Companies, Inc. Cheektowaga, New York.

Library of Congress Cataloging-in-Publication Data

National Geographic's driving guides to America. Canada / prepared by the Book Division, National Geographic Society.
p. cm.
Includes index.
ISBN 0-7922-3428-6
1. Canada—Tours. 2. Automobile travel—Canada—Guidebooks. I. National Geographic Society (U.S.). Book Division.
F1009.N38 1997
917.104'648--dc21 96-29758
CIP

Visit the Society's Web site at www.nationalgeographic.com